LEAN, LONG & STRONG

LEAN, LONG & STRONG

THE 6-WEEK STRENGTH-TRAINING, FAT-BURNING PROGRAM FOR WOMEN

WINI LINGUVIC

COAUTHOR OF THE *New York Times* BESTSELLER *BodyChange*

FOREWORD BY MONTEL WILLIAMS

RODALE

© 2005 by Wini Linguvic
Photographs © 2005 by Rodale Inc.

All rights reserved. No part of this publication may be reproduced or transmitted in any form or by any means, electronic or mechanical, including photocopying, recording, or any other information storage and retrieval system, without the written permission of the publisher.

Printed in the United States of America
Rodale Inc. makes every effort to use acid-free ∞, recycled paper ♻.

Interior photographs by Mitch Mandel

Book design by Christina Gaugler

Library of Congress Cataloging-in-Publication Data

Linguvic, Wini.
    Lean, long, and strong : the 6-week strength-training, fat-burning program for women / Wini Linguvic ; foreword by Montel Williams.
        p.   cm.
    Includes index.
    ISBN-13 978–1–57954–956–5 paperback
    ISBN-10 1–57954–956–X paperback
    ISBN-13 978–1–59486–464–3 hardcover
    ISBN-10 1–59486–464–0 hardcover
    1. Weight training for women.   2. Exercise for women.   3. Physical fitness for women.   4. Muscle strength.
I. Title.
GV546.6.W64L56   2005
613.7'045—dc22   2004018459

Distributed to the trade by Holtzbrinck Publishers

      6 8 10 9 7   paperback
2 4 6 8 10 9 7 5 3   hardcover

WE **INSPIRE** AND **ENABLE** PEOPLE TO IMPROVE
THEIR LIVES AND THE WORLD AROUND THEM

FOR MORE OF OUR PRODUCTS
WWW.RODALESTORE.COM
(800) 848-4735

For all the women who are just beginning
to discover how strong they truly are.

CONTENTS

FOREWORD

If you're like me, you can count on one hand, maybe two, the number of people who've changed your life. And if your list is like mine, it probably includes your spouse, your kids, a favorite teacher, a dear relative, your mentor, and your best friend. But I have someone on my list that I don't think most people do—my personal trainer. I started working out with Wini Linguvic 9 years ago when she introduced me to a fitness philosophy that mirrored my own approach to life. She said that if you believe in yourself, take control of your mind and body, and go outside of your comfort zone, you can move any mountain.

Since we've begun working out together, that mountain has been everything from bench-pressing 10 pounds more than I ever thought I could to living with the challenges, pains, and fears brought on by multiple sclerosis. In 2001, Wini and I wrote the book *BodyChange,* demonstrating how you can change your body in 21 days. We firmly believe that's all it takes to begin changing how you look *to* the world. But of equal or even greater benefit is that it changes how you look *at* the world.

Now Wini has designed a precision strength-training program especially for women, and if she's not already on the list of people who have changed your life, I guarantee she will be when you start using this book. No list should be complete without her. But keep in mind that there's only one person who could ever be at the top of that list—that's *you!* If you're reading this book, you've already taken the first step. And with Wini in your corner, you're well on your way.

Montel Williams

PART ONE

THE SMART WAY
TO GET FIT FAST

WORK OUT SMARTER, NOT HARDER

In case you're wondering, I'm here to give you some answers:

Yes, you can be strong *and* be graceful.

Yes, you can get fit *and* still have time for the rest of your life.

Yes, you can enjoy a workout that makes you feel energized and balanced, *and* sculpts lean, long muscles.

Now, how about some questions: Have you been doing the same workouts for weeks or even months without getting noticeable results? Did you work out regularly in the past, but now feel like you have too little time—or energy—to devote to exercise? Have you been spending a lot of time doing cardio workouts, but you're still waiting for your body to improve? Do you love how stretch class or Pilates makes you feel but also want to sculpt your body or firm up certain trouble spots?

If you answered yes to any of these questions, it's time to shake up the way you look at your exercise goals. It's time to work out smarter, not harder.

LEAN, LONG, AND STRONG: THE NEW "RECIPE" FOR FITNESS

As a personal trainer for more than 20 years, I have had the opportunity to observe a lot of people as they work out. And I've noticed a frequent pattern: Despite showing up at the gym regularly and completing demanding workouts, many women are getting minimal returns for their efforts. Their bodies don't change. Stomachs don't get flatter. Legs don't get leaner. Arms don't get cut and toned. Yet, amazingly, these women don't question their workouts. Instead, they blame *themselves,* believing that they're somehow at fault for not working out hard enough or long enough.

I say it's time to place the blame where it really belongs: *on the workout.* After all, if you had a recipe for Cajun fish and it tasted terrible every time you tried it, wouldn't you conclude that the recipe was flawed? Well, perhaps the "recipe" you've been following for flat abs, a firm butt, or shapely legs is flawed as well. In fact, if you're concentrating on just one aspect of fitness, I can guarantee you that it is.

When most women choose an exercise program, they pick a cardio (also known as aerobic) activity, such as walking, running, Spinning, or working out on a stairclimber or rowing machine. Cardio workouts are great for you, no doubt about it. They strengthen your heart and lungs, burn calories, and increase your endurance. But the truth is, they can do only so much; they can't sculpt your body, increase your flexibility, or improve your strength and posture.

Likewise, many women are devoted to their stretching or mind-body classes. Stretching lengthens your muscles, making you more flexible and graceful. But it doesn't burn a lot of calories or fat, and it doesn't give your cardiovascular system a workout. And while mind-body classes offer a great meditative aspect and teach you to connect to your breath, their potential for reshaping the body is limited.

Finally, there's strength training, which is using some form of resistance, such as dumbbells or your body weight, to challenge and build muscle. Unfortunately, strength training (also known as weight training) seems to suffer from bad P.R. Somehow, women got the notion that working out with weights would leave them looking like Arnold Schwarzenegger. As a result, very few women do it, but those who do find that it sculpts and firms up their bodies in a way that nothing else can. But as good as it is, it doesn't improve your endurance, increase your lung capacity, or necessarily make you more flexible and graceful.

When you focus on just one kind of workout, you get limited results. To truly get the most out of your workouts—and get the sculpted, trim, flexible body we all want—you need a new approach.

Perhaps you've heard the buzzword *synergy*. Synergy is the phenomenon that occurs when certain actions are combined at strategic moments, and the results are far greater than the sum of their parts.

Whereas regular exercise is about addition—20 crunches plus 20 more crunches equals a lot of time—my program is about using synergy to multiply the power of your workouts. You'll take the best of strength training, cardio work, and stretching and integrate them into fat-blasting, muscle-sculpting routines that yield maximum results in minimum time. In fact, my program is built on workouts that take only about 12 minutes, 4 days a week. Add in 20 minutes or so of a cardio activity 3 days a week, and you're on your way to achieving a whole new level of fitness.

Instead of *just* burning calories, or *just* increasing flexibility, or *just* defining your muscles, my synergistic workouts will help you achieve all three. After all, we deserve all three. A fit, healthy body is lean, long *and* strong.

The Ultimate in Synergy

The single most revolutionary aspect of the Lean, Long, and Strong program is its unique integration of stretches with strength-training exercises to help you reap the benefits of synergy. Each workout is made up of a special combination of moves grouped into what I call *synergy sets*. In each of these sets, you'll do precise strength-training exercises followed immediately by specially chosen stretches that make the strength-training move you just completed even more effective. Your muscles will become longer and stronger than they

Balance: The Key to Changing Your Body

Changing your body requires balance. Not the double pirouette kind of balance you see Olympic ice-skaters exhibit (*Oh my, I can't look, she's going to fall!*). Not the handstand away from the wall (*Is he kidding?*) kind of balance that my yoga teacher can do. The balance required to transform your body starts with your exercise program.

Simply put, balance is the state in which all the various elements come together to form a satisfying whole, without one piece being out of proportion or overemphasized. As great as it sounds, "balance" doesn't get a lot of media attention. Instead, we hear about extremes: the new workout program that requires you to work out for 3 hours a day. The fad diet that promises you can lose 50 pounds in a month. The "incredible" exercise contraption that magically works your muscles for you.

It's tough to stay centered in this world of extremes. The problem with diets and trendy workout programs is that they create impossible standards that set you up for failure. We're led into an "all-or-nothing" way of thinking, as we promise ourselves, "I will work out every day no matter what" or "I will banish all high-calorie foods from my life forever" or "I will exercise for 2 hours today and not a minute less."

Taking such an all-or-nothing approach with yourself is like walking on a tightrope—one wrong move and everything's lost. You won't be able to stay balanced with such a shaky plan. And when you fall (as would if you'd done the exercises by themselves.

How do I know that the synergy sets are effective? I see the results every day—in my own body and the bodies of my clients. I developed synergy sets over the course of years, through trial and error, as I revised and reworked my individual exercise program to get the best results.

The story of how I developed synergy sets is also in great part the story of my career as a professional trainer. When I first started training at 16 years old, I made a lot of common mistakes. I trained legs every day, ignored my upper body, and spent way too much time doing aerobics. Over the years, I learned everything I could about getting into shape and began sharing my love of fitness with others, first by teaching classes and then by becoming a personal trainer. I've had the pleasure of working with some amazing clients as I helped them reach their fitness goals. And a number of years ago, I wrote the best-selling book *Body-*

Change with one of these clients—and an extraordinary human being—Montel Williams. Since then, I've continued to try out new forms of exercise, but I keep coming back to the same conclusion: Strength training changes bodies best.

I started incorporating more stretching into my routine a few years ago because I wanted to increase my level of flexibility for yoga. Previously, I had always rushed through a few quick stretches at the end of the workout. I wanted to maximize my time in the gym, so instead of adding more stretches at the end of my workout, I decided to integreate them between sets of strength-training exercises that I was already doing. The stretches felt so good that I kept adding more. Instead of resting between exercises, I now spent that time stretching. Holding a stretch for 30 seconds was also a reminder to focus on my breathing and not on what was on my desk waiting for me at home.

you've been set up to do), you get in the habit of failing. You start to feel bad and may even convince yourself that you can't stick to an exercise program, when all you had to do was try a more balanced approach.

The Lean, Long, and Strong workouts you'll be doing in this book were built on the key concept of balance. They acknowledge that you have a lot more going on in your day than just working out. So instead of 2-hour workouts, you'll be doing workouts specially designed

to get you maximum results in as little as 12 minutes a day. And if you missed your workout yesterday, you don't need to give up; just pick up where you left off. Instead of setting you up for failure, these workouts make success seem easy.

Best of all, by combining strength training, cardio work, and stretching, the plan gives you an effective, fast, and practical approach to balancing all your needs: You will become lean, long, and strong. You'll enjoy a trim, sculpted body; feel more agile and

graceful; and get through your day more easily, feeling strong and energized. Plus, bringing balance into your workouts will make you more self-aware and more confident. And when you apply this awareness to other aspects of your life, those areas that are not in balance will become more visible, which means you can apply the same principles to them. Ultimately, you won't set yourself up to fail by reaching for extremes, but you will find yourself balancing on the strength of your successes.

Quickly, I started seeing the benefits of my integrated workouts. Stretching between sets of an exercise took me to the next level of connecting to my body. After 20 years of lifting weights, which I loved, I was able to dial in on a whole new level of fitness by integrating the best stretches with the most efficient strength-training exercises. The intensity of my entire workout increased as one movement flowed to the next. Plus, it felt phenomenal. I could literally feel the energy flowing through me.

Stretching helps you connect your breath to your body, and I found that the focus on my breathing calmed me down and helped me focus even more intently on the workout. The lengthening stretches not only felt great, but when I did the next set of strength-training exercises, I could feel the exercises in greater depth. It was the difference between looking quickly at a painting in passing and taking a moment to experience the vibrant colors. I like to think of it as "training in color"—integrating stretches throughout my workout brought a whole new dimension to the experience.

Best of all, I discovered that I reaped benefits all day from those few extra moments spent stretching in between sets of an exercise. My mind was calmer, and my body felt even better than it had with my old workouts.

To give my clients the same amazing benefits, I started integrating complementary stretching (stretches that directly correspond with the muscles being worked) into their workouts. For instance, if we did an intensive exercise for the glutes such as a lunge, we would follow that immediately with a great stretch for the glutes. Benefits came right away. Their routines flowed easily, they had less soreness after a workout, and they maximized their results with a minimum of time invested. Inches were lost, clothes fit better, and slouching was replaced by walking tall. Their legs looked longer and their abdominals and arms were better defined. My clients also told me they could feel, or connect to, their bodies better with the integrated strengthening and stretching. And the added stretches along with the focus on the breath helped prevent injury and brought them a sense of calm.

After seeing these results in my clients, I knew I needed to share these routines in a program designed just for women. Women—with their quest for leaner legs, firmer glutes, flatter stomachs, and more-toned arms—need a commonsense workout that *works*. You now hold that program in your hands, and with it, the detailed map to getting lean, long, and strong in workouts of just 12 minutes.

MORE "SECRETS" FOR SUCCESS

While the cornerstone of my workout program is the synergy set, that's not the only unique feature. You'll also get maximum results in minimum time with the following core features of the program.

Customized plans to target key trouble spots. We all have them: those areas of our bodies that we'd particularly like to tone up. Maybe you've just had a baby, and you really want to firm up your abs. Or maybe summer's coming, and you'd like to tone up those thighs so you look great when you wear a pair of shorts. In part three of the book, I'll give you specific focus programs to target key trouble zones. And if your goal is all-around fitness, you'll also find a total-body, fat-blasting program that will give you amazing results.

Precision combination of compound and isolation moves. You'll also enjoy the benefits that come with the unique design of each workout routine. Each set of strength-training exercises builds on the previous one, combining a mix of compound and isolation movements, which more effectively sculpt your body. For example, in the lower-body workouts, you'll do standing exercises followed by targeted leg exercises done while lying on the floor. This way, your muscles have already been challenged by the time you start the floorwork, and there's no need for dozens of ineffective reps.

Strength Training: Debunking the Myths

Where the belief that women shouldn't lift weights got started, we'll never know. Maybe we saw teenage boys lifting weights and growing like weeds, and we assumed the same would happen to us. Somewhere along the line, many of us developed the belief that lifting dumbbells would immediately turn us into a female version of the Incredible Hulk. Let's take a closer look at the three most common reasons women usually give for not doing strength-training exercises.

I don't want to get big. This is the most common excuse, but I'm here to tell you it's just not going to happen. Even if you wanted to develop big muscles, it's pretty difficult for a woman to get big and bulky from weight training.

Sure, there are lots of male bodybuilders who have huge, superhero-like muscles. But women don't have the kind of hormones a man has. Our muscles cannot get as big. The women you may see on TV who are bodybuilders have devoted hours each day for many years to working out and some-times have manipulated their hormones to purposefully gain muscle.

Getting big does not happen by accident. You don't do a set of lateral raises to sculpt your shoulders and the next day find it impossible to fit through a doorway without going sideways. And actually, even a lot of men find it hard to get big. They're the ones who have all the hormones to gain muscle, and they don't wake up the day after their workouts and get stuck in their doorways either.

I don't want to get muscle-bound. Again, not a concern with my balanced workouts.

Is it possible to get muscle-bound? If all you do is lift really heavy weights for a very limited range of motion—and that is *all* you do—sure, it could be a challenge to reach over and touch your toes. But the right strength-training exercises actually increase your flexibility. The exercises you'll be doing require you to move your muscles through their full range of motion, so the muscles get stretched as well as strengthened. Plus, each synergy set includes at least one specific stretch, virtually eliminating any chance that you'll become muscle-bound.

I should lose weight first. I don't want to turn my fat into muscle. I understand wanting to put off something until you feel better about yourself. We've all done it. Here's the catch with this one, though.

Muscle and fat are two different things. Fat doesn't turn into muscle and muscle doesn't turn into fat. I know you're thinking about that retired football player who can't fit into his custom-made suits anymore. Well, his muscle didn't turn into fat. He simply stopped training, so his muscles got smaller. At the same time, he started gaining body fat because he didn't have anything to do in his retirement except watch old football films and eat ice cream.

Fat won't turn to muscle. But having more muscle can help you lose fat. Strength training will *help* you lose weight. Not only will it not get in the way of any diet or weight-loss strategy you have, but having more muscle on your body will increase your metabolism, helping you to burn more calories even when you're at rest.

Maximum toning with an exercise ball.
Many of the exercises are designed to be done while sitting or lying on an exercise ball. By using the ball, not only do you work the target muscles, but your abdominals and lower back also are challenged as they keep you in balance and in good form. With every move, you are challenging the muscles of your core, which include the abdominals, obliques (your waistline), and the all-important lower back. By doing exercises at a variety of angles—such as when sitting or lying on a ball—your body gets stronger using all the muscles *together,* the way they're used in real life.

Effective weight work. My workouts use weights in a way that allows you to get maximum results in a minimum amount of time. If you've taken toning or body sculpting classes geared toward women, you've probably noticed that almost all of them emphasize doing a high number of reps with very light weights. But this ignores an important fact: The best way to define the muscles is to challenge them. And unfortunately, using light weights to do endless reps is simply not enough of a challenge.

I spent many years teaching a class called Cuts. Women of all ages, shapes, and sizes would attend, including pregnant women, women over 40, dancers, and even grandmothers. Unlike traditional toning classes that used very light weights for endless repetitions, I had everyone using weights that were challenging for just 15 reps per set. Though some of the women were intimidated at first by the fear that they'd get big, that fear was soon replaced by the wonderful feeling of being strong. And as other women started seeing the results my students were getting, they began venturing into the class, too.

The body responds to the challenge of a heavier weight by getting stronger. So instead of using light weights to do hundreds of reps that

challenge your patience but not your body, my workout program encourages you to use whatever weight is a challenge for you to lift for just 15 reps. In other words, you'll challenge your muscles not by seeing how many reps you can do, but by seeing how *few* reps you can do.

At-home convenience. Because the workouts don't require complex exercise machines, you can do them at home any time you get 12 minutes to spare. There's no need to go to a gym or purchase expensive exercise equipment. Your workouts will be more convenient to do, so it will be easier to integrate them into your day.

ROUNDING OUT YOUR WORKOUTS

As amazing as the workouts are, to take full advantage of them—to become truly lean, long, and strong—you need to balance them with cardio work and eating right.

Count on cardio. Though it's strength training that will sculpt your body and give your muscles definition, cardio exercise is still important. After all, the most important muscle in your body is your heart. No one dies of weak biceps. So I encourage you to supplement your strength training and stretching with a 20-minute cardio workout 3 days a week. You don't need to do anything elaborate: Walking, swimming, cycling, even jumping rope will do. Later in the book, I'll give you an easy-to-follow plan that will allow you to add in some cardio training easily and efficiently.

Use the kitchen to support your workouts. What you put into your body makes a big difference in the strength and energy you get out of it. For that reason, an entire section of this book is devoted to evaluating your daily eating habits and developing a balanced approach to food. Notice that I didn't say the word *diet.* I believe that because diets hold you up to a rigid standard, they set you up for failure. Plus, most diets these days have you eliminate major food groups, and that approach just doesn't work for the long term.

Instead of a diet, I'm going to give you practical strategies you can use to substitute healthy eating habits for unhealthy ones. Each week for 6 weeks—exactly the amount of time it will take you to complete one level of the Lean, Long, and Strong workouts—I'll ask you to try some new strategies that will support your workouts nutritionally. You can combine these commonsense strategies to meet your individual goals, needs, and taste preferences to come up with a plan that works for you.

What Benefits Can You Expect?

For most of us, fat loss is at the top of our fitness goals. And for this, you can't do better than the balanced workouts in this book. To understand why, you'll need to know a little bit about physiology.

Scientists know that muscle tissue burns more calories than fat tissue does, even when you're at rest. So the more lean muscle you have, the better your metabolism works. This means that if you have two women who both weigh 140 pounds, but one has more muscle than the other, the woman with more muscle will burn more calories than her friend, even when they're both just sitting around watching TV.

Unfortunately, women naturally lose muscle mass as they age. This makes their metabolism slow down—and the scale creep higher. The solution? Strength training. Simply put, it's the best way to preserve muscle.

Yes, it's true that your metabolism increases while you do cardio exercise. But what many people don't realize is that it increases only for the amount of time you're working out. So, if you walk on a treadmill for 45 minutes, your metabolism will speed up for those 45 minutes, but no longer. On the other hand, if you focus on exercises that preserve muscle mass—such as the ones in this book—your metabolism will be working better all the time, not just while you're exercising.

Yet fat loss is not the only benefit you'll gain from the strength-training exercises in this book. After all, it's called *strength* training for a reason. With these workouts, you'll get physically stronger, which means you'll be able to accomplish more in your day. You'll have better posture, get through your chores and errands more easily, improve your joint strength, and experience fewer body aches and pains. You can have this strength without a bulky physique. Women are meant to be strong, and the right exercises will give you the lean, long, and strong look of a fit woman.

By integrating your strength-training moves with stretching, you'll become more flexible—and more graceful. You'll gain a greater sense of connectedness to your entire body. As a result, you'll be able to do all other forms of activity better. And because you'll improve your range of motion, you will limit your chances for straining a muscle as you go about your day.

And finally, by incorporating the concept of "flow" into your exercise routines—by moving through the exercises, one right after the other—you will be gaining some of the cardiovascular benefits of an aerobic workout. When you supplement this with a few cardio workouts each week, you will decrease your risk for a heart attack or cardiovascular disease, gain stamina, and burn calories.

The time has come for a change. It's time to redefine fitness—and to stop settling for less than the whole. Fitness means endurance, flexibility, *and* strength. And with the precision workouts in this book, you will gain all three.

MAKING THE PROGRAM WORK FOR YOU

Imagine yourself lean, long, and strong. You note your progress by your defined legs, toned arms, and flat abs. You feel strong and energetic, able to get through your day effortlessly. Whether you're carrying groceries, running to catch the bus to work, or simply opening a jar of pickles, things that once wore you out are now no problem. You run up stairs that used to leave you breathless, you're standing taller, and you've even noticed that the lower-back pain that was becoming your constant companion has completely disappeared.

Just by opening this book, you've already taken the first step to making this vision a reality. And fortunately, the Lean, Long, and Strong Program is so simple, you don't need to spend a lot of time figuring out what you're going to be doing or finding and buying expensive gym equipment. All of the exercises can be done at home, with minimal equipment and about 12 minutes, 3 or 4 days a week.

Let's begin by running through the equipment you'll need. Then I'll explain how the exercise programs are set up, and then . . . it's time to get working so you can make your vision a reality!

THE GEAR

You may already have some of the gear you'll need lying around your house. Or you might be able to borrow it from a friend. But even if you need to buy it new, you can find all of the equipment at any sporting goods store, and the cost should be minimal. You can also log on to www.LeanLongandStrong.com for more information and other resources. Here's what you'll need.

Dumbbells. You'll want to have a set of dumbbells handy. For a lot of the exercises (such as pushups and walking lunges), you'll begin by using your own body weight as the resistance. Gradually,

though, you'll be integrating dumbbells into your routine. Metal or neoprene, painted silver or coated with rubber, the choice is yours. The most important thing is that the weights aren't too heavy or too light. When you're trying out the dumbbells, see if you can curl the weight 15 times. (Hold the dumbbells with your arms close to your sides, palms facing forward, then bring them up toward your shoulders.) If this is way too easy, choose a weight that's a few pounds heavier. If it's difficult to do even a few repetitions, choose a lighter weight. You will be gradually working up to using heavier weights, so it's best to have at least three sets of dumbbells of different weights. A set of 5, 8, and 10 pounds is a great place to start for most women. If you have already done some strength training, you can start out with 8, 10, and 12 pounds.

Another great option is to purchase an adjustable dumbbell set called PowerBlocks. With these, you can easily change the weight of the dumbbells without buying different sizes of weights. Many sporting goods stores carry PowerBlocks, and they can also be purchased online.

An exercise ball. You will need a stability ball, also known as an exercise ball. A stability ball gives you a surface to lie, sit, or lean on. In fact, just sitting on a ball can feel great for your back. I call it "active sitting" because your body is constantly adjusting to keep you balanced on the unstable surface of the ball. Because the ball isn't stable, your body has to be.

There are two kinds of stability balls: physio-rolls and round exercise balls, also called Swiss balls. A physioroll is a larger ball that looks almost like two balls molded together. Like a traditional round exercise ball, it provides an unstable surface for you to lie on sideways, facedown, or faceup. The difference is that instead of being totally unstable like the round ball, it rolls only forward and backward for moderate instability.

A round, or Swiss, ball will also work great in these routines, although it will be very challenging from the start because of its instability. I prefer the physioroll for the beginner. It provides greater stability and allows you to do more variations of exercises. For example, many women can do Swiss ball crunches on the round ball but find the more advanced exercises (such as a roll-in or side crunch) too challenging. With a physioroll, you can be challenged yet still feel a bit more stable. Of course, if you are advanced, you can do all of these exercises on a traditional round ball. (For more on physiorolls, see page 39.)

A mat. You will need a comfortable and firm surface to lie on. Having some padding under you allows you to focus on the exercises. If the area where you'll be working out is carpeted, you should be fine. If not, buy an exercise mat. Mats are available in sporting goods stores as well as department stores.

A towel. Any standard-size towel you have in your linen closet will do. You'll be using it to complete some of the exercises, so if you also like to have a towel handy to wipe your face as you work out, you might want to have a separate one for that.

Water. You'll want to have a water bottle nearby so you can easily drink water before, during, and after your workout. Keep drinking at regular intervals throughout your workout to prevent de-

Outwit Your Fitness Obstacles

Henry Ford once said, "Obstacles are those frightful things you see when you take your eyes off your goal." When it comes to finding the time, energy, or motivation to exercise, there are always going to be obstacles. See if any of the following sound familiar to you.

"I'll start exercising next month. I'll be ready then." The future isn't tangible, so it's easy to dump your goals there to deal with when next month comes. Yet next month is always that: *next* month.

I've found in speaking with people about their fitness goals that they're always talking about getting started. They tell me they'll begin when everything comes to-gether, when the timing is right. They'll start working out after the holidays. Or on Monday, or Friday, or their birthday, or—perhaps the most popular one—New Year's Day.

We could wait forever if we wait till the right time. There will always be something going on, some obligation we need to fulfill, or some place we need to be. The truth is, there is never a "perfect" time when all conditions are ideal. The right time is now. If you wait until all circumstances are perfect, you will be waiting endlessly.

I remember going to my aunt's house as a child. She had just had a baby, and she had every baby accessory you could imagine, or at least so it seemed to my young eyes. The freshly painted nursery and brightly colored toys for my new cousin were little luxuries that were new to me. As we left her home, I remember saying to my father, "I want to have all those things when I have a child. I want to be able to give him everything."

"Then you will always wait," my father said. "You will never feel ready if you wait for the perfect situation. You will never feel like you have enough money. And then life will pass you by."

My father raised three children on a bookkeeper's salary. I'm glad he didn't wait until he was ready.

"I'm too busy." The workouts in

hydration. The best way to keep yourself well-hydrated is to drink water before you feel thirsty.

Workout clothes and shoes. Since the workouts can be done at home, there's no need to invest in an elaborate workout wardrobe. In fact, I usually work out in a tank top and a simple pair of shorts. Wear whatever's comfortable for you, as long as you can move easily and comfortably. Just don't wear anything too loose or heavy that could get in the way of the exercises. As for shoes, your best option is a sturdy pair of cross-trainers. The support they offer is especially good for the standing exercises. Tennis, running, or walking shoes will also give you the support you need if you have those already.

A training log. Following each workout, you'll find a blank training log. There are also blank logs without photos beginning on page 286. I recommend making a few photocopies of the logs for the workouts you'll be doing and then gathering them into a binder. As you do each exercise or stretch, record the number of reps or breaths you've completed. Then, the next time you do the same workout, you'll know what you need to do to improve upon your previous workout.

Understanding the Lean, Long, and Strong Program

Each exercise and stretch that I recommend is explained step by step in part two of the book. If this book take only about 12 minutes a day. They can be done in your home, and there are even express alternatives for the days you are traveling or really rushed.

I firmly believe that if you have days when you can't find 12 minutes for yourself, those are the days when you need to find 30. The busier you are, the more you need to take a few minutes for yourself. Exercise is the ultimate stress reliever.

"I'm too tired." Exercise reduces fatigue. Anyone who exercises regularly knows that. But that's preaching to the converted. The hardest part is picking yourself up and starting. The good news is that by following one of the basic programs, you'll slowly introduce exercise into your life and gradually be able to make it part of your routine. You may soon discover that you feel more tired on the days you don't work out!

"I can't get motivated." I think a lot of people have the wrong idea of what motivation is. They think it's some magic potion that will show up at their door, and all of a sudden they'll exercise, clean the house, and dry the dishes. I wait and wait for the motivation to dry the dishes, but it just never comes. The dishes just sit there until I get up and dry them whether I feel like it or not. Sometimes I ask the dog to dry them, but greyhounds aren't motivated to do anything but sleep and look cute.

We can't wait for motivation to happen. We need to begin even on the days we think we can't. Yet when we decide to begin, something amazing happens—it seems the whole world aligns with our goals. All of a sudden, doing gets easier. Not by wishing to be motivated. But by actually *doing*.

There's a great quote on my desk that I think people of all religions and beliefs can appreciate: "Begin to weave and God will provide the thread." Motivation comes by doing. We begin, and then it gets easier because we have already begun. So don't wait for motivation to come to your door. Go out and meet it.

you flip to that section (beginning on page 23), you'll see that the moves are grouped by the part of the body they work, starting with the core and moving on to the lower body, followed by the upper body. Each group—core, lower body, and upper body—contains a basic workout for beginners, an intermediate workout, a challenge workout, and an express workout. These workouts are the building blocks upon which the exercise programs in part three of the book are constructed. But before we discuss how those workouts are used in part three, let's take a closer look at the exercises themselves.

Precision Exercises, Customized for You

Have you ever bought one of those cute little cotton T-shirts with a label inside that says "one size fits all"? They usually look really good on the shelf, but to be honest, I don't know anyone who can wear those tiny tops. Well, on second thought, my 4-year-old niece can wear anything. She has great style, that niece of mine.

Most likely, if you did purchase one of those T-shirts, I'll bet you discovered it just didn't fit right. Maybe the arms were too tight or it was too small across the chest. Either way, it didn't really work for you, and you wound up feeling as if you somehow weren't the right size.

The truth is, one size does *not* fit all. One size does not even fit most. Likewise, there is no one-size-fits-all workout program. We are all built differently and come to the exercises with different abilities.

Perhaps the last time you got any "real" exercise was the kickball game you played in the fifth grade. Or maybe you used to be a dedicated gym rat but gave up your workouts a couple of years ago when your job became more demanding.

Perhaps you used to take dance classes or played on the school tennis team or have always been naturally flexible. Each of us is unique, and each of us has special strengths as well as areas that are challenges for us.

For that reason, I'll give you special instructions for the strength-training exercises and stretches that allow you to adjust the move to match your ability. Simply look for the "One Size Does Not Fit All" label. Here you'll find tips to simplify the exercise if you're a beginner. And if you find that the exercise isn't challenging enough for you, you'll find ways to increase the difficulty.

After you've been doing an exercise for a few weeks and are feeling comfortable with it, I invite you to try the more challenging version. This way, you can progress at your own pace, and you can take pride in seeing how far you've come.

PUTTING IT ALL TOGETHER

Now that you've been introduced to the exercises and workouts in part two, it's time to see how they all come together in part three. While you can certainly pick and choose from the exercises on your own, for maximum effectiveness, it's best to choose one of the four basic workout programs presented in part three. If you haven't been working out regularly, I recommend that you choose the Fat-Blasting Focus Program, beginning with the basic level. This program will improve your overall fitness by working out your entire body. It's a great way to add some activity into your day, and you'll get to try out the basic workouts for the core, lower body, and upper body. Best of all, in just 6 weeks, you'll notice visible changes: Your body will be firming up, you'll begin to see hints of curves where you once lacked muscle definition, and you'll undoubtedly have more energy.

If you have already been working out fairly regularly, you might want to skip ahead to the intermediate level of the Fat-Blasting Focus Program. As you would expect, this program is built by doing the more difficult, intermediate workouts from part two of the book. You'll challenge your body and build muscle definition as you complete the intermediate level of the core, lower-body, and upper-body workouts.

Once you've completed either the 6-week basic or 6-week intermediate Fat-Blasting Focus Program, you may decide to continue on with the next level of this program—intermediate if you completed the basic level, challenge level if you completed the intermediate one. Or, you have the option at this point to concentrate your workouts on a key trouble zone for you. To do this, simply choose the program from part three that you'd like to focus on: Core, Lower-Body, or Upper-Body.

Even if you decide to customize at this point, you're still going to be getting a full-body workout. You can think of my focus programs as putting an "accent" on your chosen trouble spot. So, for example, if your goal is to get toned, shapely arms that will look great in a sundress, you'll follow the Upper-Body Focus Program. You'll still do one lower-body and one core

workout each week, but you'll double up on your upper-body workouts. Start with the basic level for 6 weeks. By then, you should be ready to move on to the intermediate level of the Upper-Body Focus Program, which you'll need to do for the next 6 weeks.

What if you have more than one area you'd like to focus on? In this age of multitasking, it might seem strange not to work on more than one problem area at once. But I strongly encourage you to choose just one fitness goal to focus on at a time. Why? Well, if your program remains the same, then what changes is *you*. During the 6 weeks you devote to a particular Focus program, you'll get stronger as you adapt to the program. Whether through better form, increased resistance, or an extra breath in each stretch, you are the one changing as the program remains the same. If you change the program before giving it a chance, you have no mirror. You have nothing to measure your progress by. But by sticking to a program for 6 weeks, you get to watch yourself improve.

Of course, once you've completed the 6 weeks and reached your first fitness goal, you can either progress to a more advanced program for that focus area or move on to other areas of your body that you want to tone and strengthen. And by then, you'll have the additional motivation that comes with seeing a goal through to its end.

PRECISION CARDIO

Of all the muscles in your body,

the heart is the most important. And like any other muscle, the way to strengthen your heart is to challenge it. Cardio (also known as aerobic) exercise increases your heart's ability to pump blood and your lungs' ability to provide oxygen to the rest of the body. This improved heart and lung power means that you can climb a long flight of stairs without getting winded or play with your kids in the park without having to take a break on the bench. It also means that you reduce your risk for having a heart attack or developing cardiovascular disease. And by revving up your metabolism, cardiovascular exercise helps to accelerate fat-burning. Plus, it just plain feels good.

I recommend that you do a 20-minute cardio workout three times a week. You can do it on the same day as your synergy set workout or save it for one of your "off" days. If you choose to do it on the same day as your synergy set workout, you can do the workouts at different times of the day, say one in the morning and one in the afternoon, or do them consecutively. One size does *not* fit all; figure out a schedule that works for your busy life. And remember: The days you can't find 20 minutes to exercise are the days you deserve it most.

SPIN, SWIM, OR JOG: THE CHOICE IS YOURS

Many people ask me what I think the best type of cardio exercise is for them. My answer is always the same: The best cardio exercise for you is the kind that you will actually do. If you're going to stick with your exercise routine, you've got to pick an activity that you enjoy. For inspiration, you might want to think back to what you enjoyed doing as a child. Did you love the sensation of riding your bike down your neighborhood street,

the wind blowing your hair as you zipped along? Then maybe it's time to get pedaling once again. Is grabbing a jump rope and sneaking in 20 minutes of exercise while you watch the evening news more your speed? That's a fine form of cardiovascular exercise, too. Or maybe you've always loved the simplicity of jogging. If so, there's no time like the present to strap on those running shoes and go explore your neighborhood.

My only caution is to make sure you choose a form of exercise that works for your body. If not, you risk injury. For example, running can be very stressful to the body. If you have back or knee problems, you might want to choose a more gentle activity, such as walking or swimming.

Here's a list of the cardio exercises I recommend, since you can do them on your own and they don't involve a lot of starting and stopping, unlike activities such as playing softball or tennis.

◆ Walking
◆ Jogging alternating with walking
◆ Swimming
◆ Cycling outdoors
◆ Stationary cycling
◆ Using a stairclimber
◆ Using an elliptical machine
◆ Jumping rope
◆ Using a rowing machine

If you're just starting an exercise program and are unsure which cardio activity to choose, I recommend walking. Easy on the joints, it can be done anywhere. And taking a 20-minute walk during the day is a great way to relieve stress.

Of course, feel free to mix up your cardio workouts. Maybe you'll want to walk some days, cycle others. Or perhaps you'll find that changing up your cardio workouts with swimming, jumping rope, and using the rowing machine keeps you motivated. This is fine and leaves you less prone to injury as well as boredom. Just have fun!

How Hard Should I Work?

When it comes to cardiovascular exercise, a common mistake is working too hard. For example, we've all seen people at the health club who increase the speed on the stairclimbing machines so much that it's impossible for them to stay upright in correct alignment without falling off. So they hold on to the railing for dear life as they do these teeny-tiny steps over and over again. The worst is when they're holding on *and* leaning to one side. They're either straining their

Using a Heart Rate Monitor

If you want to get more exact with your precision cardio, you can use a heart rate monitor in addition to evaluating your rate of perceived exertion. The heart rate monitor will tell you exactly what your heart rate is as you're exercising, which means you can then increase or decrease your intensity to get a precise workout. Monitors are available at sporting goods stores and some department stores.

First, you'll need to figure out the heart rate range that you should be working at. The best way to do this is to get tested by an exercise physiologist. If you don't want to do that, you can get a pretty good estimate by calculating your maximum heart rate and then calculating certain percentages of this rate to work at for your warmup and cooldown, your moderate pace, and your interval pace. This will be a good starting point, though keep in mind that this calculation is based on the "average" person—

something that none of us is!

To estimate your maximum heart rate, subtract your age from 226. (Men would subtract their age from 220.)

226 − your age = age-adjusted maximum heart rate

Now, take your age-adjusted maximum heart rate and calculate the following percentages for the various parts of your workout.

◆ 60 percent for your warmup and cooldown
◆ 65 to 75 percent for your moderate pace
◆ 75 to 85 percent for your vigorous or interval pace

For instance, a 40-year-old woman's estimated maximum heart rate is 186 (226 − 40 = 186).

60 percent of her max = 112
65 percent of her max = 121

75 percent of her max = 140
85 percent of her max = 158

Keep in mind, however, that this calculation can be off by as much as 15 beats, so use the rate of perceived exertion as well. Also take into account that your heart rate can vary depending on which activity you choose. Different activities use different skills and muscle groups, so an experienced swimmer will have a lower heart rate swimming than she does when running. Keep that in mind as you vary your cardio choices. Also, some exercises that you do while sitting down, like riding a recumbent bicycle, won't get your heart rate as high as those that you do while standing, such as walking hills outside. So use your heart rate monitor and evaluate your rate of perceived exertion, but also learn to listen to your body.

wrists and shoulders because they need their arms to hold them upright, or they're straining their backs because they're leaning into the machine with no regard for their posture. When we look at their 20 minutes to an hour a day spent doing cardio work this way and multiply it by three times a week for a few weeks, all those minutes of bad form add up. It's no wonder they usually end up dropping out of their exercise program due to injury.

What you do while you're exercising is a training ground for the real world. How you do anything is how you do everything. If you have bad posture on the stairclimbing machine, how is your posture going to look when you're standing in line? Good form creates more good form.

On the other hand, if you don't work out hard enough, you'll get very little benefit from your workout, and you'll probably end up dropping out because you're not seeing results. Doing an easy 20 minutes on a stationary bike while reading the morning paper and talking on your cell phone is just not enough to get results. You'll need to pick up the intensity a bit. A little more energy for the time you spend on your cardio workout really adds up.

How can you tell if you're working hard enough? A heart rate monitor will give you a very accurate way to make sure you're working within your specific target zone. (See "Using a Heart Rate Monitor.") But if you'd prefer a less high-tech method, nothing beats the convenience of simply rating your perceived exertion. Rate of perceived exertion, or RPE, on a scale from one to nine provides a standard measurement for evaluating your exercise intensity. Take a look at the chart that follows.

Rate of Perceived Exertion

Level	Feeling
1–2	Extremely easy. You can easily carry on a conversation.
3	Very easy. You can converse with almost no effort.
4	Moderately easy. You can converse with a little bit of effort.
5	Moderate. Conversation requires some effort.
6	Starting to get challenging. Conversation requires more effort.
7	Difficult. Conversation requires a lot of effort.
8	Very difficult. Conversation requires maximum effort.
9	Full-out effort. No conversation is possible.

By taking note of your perceived exertion, you can increase your intensity if you're not challenging yourself hard enough, or decrease it if you're working at a level that you can't sustain or that risks injury. For example, if you're a walker, you can increase your intensity by increasing your speed, using your arms more, or increasing the incline if you're on a treadmill or walking up hills outside.

MAKING EVERY MINUTE COUNT

By paying attention to your rate of perceived exertion, you can make sure you're using every minute of your cardio workout effectively. That way, you can get results in a total of just 60 minutes a week. Instead of spending hours on a stairclimber or not knowing how long you should be on the bike, every minute is accounted for. There's no time wasted, and every minute is put to good use.

My Precision Cardio Program consists of

three levels of workouts. I'll use walking as the example, but you can do any of the cardio exercises mentioned earlier. I recommend focusing on each level for 6 weeks. This will allow you to tie in your progress on the synergy set workouts with your cardio workouts. So, for example, if you've successfully finished 6 weeks of the Upper-Body Focus Basic Program and are ready to move on to the Upper-Body Focus Intermediate Program, you may also want to move on to the intermediate level of your Precision Cardio workout. Of course, though, one size does not fit all. If you want to stay at the basic level of cardio yet are ready to move on to the intermediate level on your upper-body workout, that's fine, too.

Also, if you've consistently been doing 20-minute cardio workouts for a minimum of 6 weeks, you might want to skip ahead to the intermediate level. However, if you're not sure which level to begin with, start with the basic. It's important to build a base of aerobic fitness before adding in interval training. By doing the basics, you're establishing a solid base to build upon.

Basic: Building a Base

When you're first starting out, the most important thing is to get moving and keep moving for 20 minutes. Start out walking for 20 minutes, 3 days a week. You will start with an easy warmup, then 10 minutes of steady walking at an RPE of 4, 5, or 6, depending on your comfort level, and finally a 5-minute easy cooldown.

Minute	Activity	RPE
1 through 5	Easy warmup	3–4
6 through 15	Moderate walking	4–5–6
16 through 20	Moderate-to-easy cooldown	3–4

Intermediate: Introduction to Interval Training

Interval training is alternating short bursts of intense movement with a short period of less-intense activity. By alternating intensity, you're training your heart to be stronger and more efficient. You get to work harder without having to increase the intensity of the entire workout.

Busting the Low-Intensity Myth

Many women choose to exercise at an extremely low intensity because they believe it will burn more fat. This idea is left over from 20 years ago when low-impact aerobics edged out its high-impact wild sister. It's true that you do burn a greater percentage of calories from fat when you exercise at a lower intensity, but you burn fewer calories overall. So window-shopping does burn a higher percentage of fat than walking vigorously, but because the total number of calories you're burning when you window-shop is low, you get limited results.

When you do your cardio work, you should be working the bulk of your time at a rate of perceived exertion of at least 4. This means you can carry on a conversation yet perhaps not belt out a Broadway tune. You should feel like your workout is an effort but that you're working at a rate you can sustain.

When you're doing your intervals, you'll be working a little harder. For example, if the prescribed interval is a level 5 rate of exertion, you should feel that although it is challenging, you can complete the interval with a bit of effort.

In the intermediate workout, you'll start with an easy warmup of 5 minutes. Then you'll do 1 minute of vigorous walking, followed by 3 minutes of less-intense walking. The workout consists of three of these intervals. As your fitness improves, you'll be able to work harder for that minute plus recover faster in between the intervals. The stronger you are, the faster you'll recover.

Minute	Activity	RPE
1 through 5	Warmup	3–4
6	Vigorous walking	5–6
7 through 9	Moderate walking	3–4
10	Vigorous walking	5–6
11 through 13	Moderate walking	3–4
14	Vigorous walking	5–6
15 through 17	Moderate walking	3–4
18 through 20	Easy cooldown	3

Challenge: Turning Up the Heat

This advanced workout increases the length of the intervals. Instead of working hard for 1 minute, you're working hard for 2. Yet the recovery time is the same. Make sure you are able to recover between intervals. If you can't recover between the intervals, take the intensity down a bit or increase the recovery time by 30 seconds.

Minute	Activity	RPE
1 through 5	Warmup	3
6 through 7	Vigorous walking	4–5–6
8 through 10	Moderate walking	3–4
11 through 12	Vigorous walking	5–6
13 through 15	Moderate walking	3–4
16 through 17	Vigorous walking	5–6
18 through 20	Moderate-to-easy cooldown	3

PART TWO

THE PRECISION WORKOUTS

DEFINING THE CORE

Core Basics

This is the first level of your midsection workout. All you need are an exercise ball (either a physio-roll or a Swiss ball), a towel, and a mat. You'll also want to have a water bottle handy so that you can drink from it as you work out. In this 10-minute workout, you'll be hitting your core from all angles, including the important lower back.

Ball Towel Crunch

STARTING POSITION

Sit upright on an exercise ball and place a rolled-up towel between your inner thighs. Walk your feet forward, letting the ball roll up your spine until it is supporting your lower back. Your head and shoulders are off the ball. Knees are in line with your ankles, and your feet are firmly on the floor. Hands are placed behind your head, and your elbows are open.

MOVEMENT

As you bring your inner thighs together to hug the towel, draw your navel into your spine. Lift your head and shoulders forward so that your rib cage moves closer to your hips. Pause at the top of the movement for 2 counts. Lower slowly and repeat. Start out with 10 perfect reps and add 1 rep with each workout until you can do 25.

The Squeeze Factor

As you begin the crunch, really draw the abs down. Imagine a sponge between your ribs and hips. Flatten it first, then wring out the excess water.

The Breath Factor

Exhale as you lift your head and shoulders and bring your ribs closer to your hips. Inhale as you lower your shoulders back to the ball.

A Word from Wini

When you're first learning this exercise, place one hand on your abs right under your ribs as you do a crunch. Feel the muscle drawing the ribs closer to the hips. Next, place your hand lower down, between your hips. It is harder to con-

One Size Does Not Fit All

BEGINNER

There are two things you can do when starting out to make this exercise easier. The first is to do it without using the towel. Instead, place your legs wide to give yourself a wider base of support. The second is to drop your hips closer to the floor by walking yourself down the ball. The side of the ball now supports your lower back and the top of the ball supports your upper back. If your hips are low enough, it will almost look like you're sitting up.

ADVANCED

Extend your arms and wrap your wrists so that your head can rest on your upper arms. By lengthening the lever of your arms, you increase the challenge.

nect to that section of the abs. Now, do the crunch, gently squeezing the towel with your inner thighs. Notice that by using the towel, it is much easier to connect to the entire length of your abdominals.

Watch Out For

When you lift your head and shoulders, focus on pressing your rib cage forward instead of raising your head up. Imagine a string pulling your ribs, not your shoulders, toward your hips.

Diagonal Ball Crunch

STARTING POSITION

Sit upright on an exercise ball and place a rolled-up towel between your inner thighs. Walk your feet forward, letting the ball roll up your spine until it is supporting your lower back. Your head and shoulders are off the ball. Knees are in line with your ankles, and your feet are firmly on the floor. Hands are placed behind your head with your elbows open.

MOVEMENT

As you bring your inner thighs together to hug the towel, draw your navel into your spine. Lift your head and shoulders forward and to the right so that your left ribs move closer to your right hip. Pause at the top of the movement for 2 counts. Lower slowly and repeat for 10 reps. Repeat on the other side for 10 reps. Add 1 rep with each workout until you can do 25.

The Squeeze Factor

Before you start moving diagonally, draw your belly button down. Squeeze the area between your ribs and the opposite hip. With every crunch, draw your abs down even more.

The Breath Factor

Exhale as you bring your ribs diagonally toward your hip. Inhale as you return to the center.

A Word from Wini

When you lift your head and shoulders, focus on decreasing the space between your rib and the opposite hip. Imagine one string pulling you forward and another of equal strength pulling you diagonally.

One Size Does Not Fit All

BEGINNER

To make the exercise easier, alternate the reps instead of doing them all on one side.

ADVANCED

Lift your right knee up to meet your left elbow, as shown. Just try one or two like this at first!

"Just get started. Then don't quit."

Watch Out For

Be careful not to tug on your neck. Make sure that both elbows stay open and that your hands are relaxed behind your head. The work is being done with the muscles of the core; the head and shoulders are merely along for the ride.

Lengthening Stretch: Hangover Break

STARTING POSITION

Sit on the exercise ball with your feet firmly placed
on the floor.

THE STRETCH

Hang over the ball and rock forward and back,
feeling the stretch in your spine. Hold for 5 slow
breaths.

The Breath Factor

As you inhale, lengthen your
spine by gently extending in
two directions, from the top
of your head to your tailbone.

As you exhale, drop your
head toward the floor and relax
your back.

A Word from Wini

Focus on your breath reaching
all the way through your body.
Notice what areas you have
tightness in that may block the
breath. Try to send your breath
to your tighter spots.

Lengthening Stretch: Drape and Stretch

STARTING POSITION

Kneel with the ball in front of you. Roll forward until the ball supports your midsection. Relax your hands and feet on the floor.

THE STRETCH

Gently rock back and forth over the ball until you find a comfortable position. Hold for 5 slow breaths.

One Size Does Not Fit All

If this is uncomfortable, try the Knees to Chest stretch (see page 55).

The Breath Factor

As you inhale, focus on increasing the space between your upper chest and lower back. As you exhale, let your body go deeper into the stretch by dropping your head and legs closer to the floor.

A Word from Wini

Find a position where you feel a nice stretch across your lower back. As the workouts pile up, experiment with having the ball higher toward your ribs or lower toward your hips. This is a great stretch to do after a long day.

Plank

STARTING POSITION

Support yourself on your forearms and your knees. Interlock your fingers and create a V shape with your forearms. Draw your shoulder blades down into your back.

HOLD POSITION

Straighten your legs out so that you are balancing on the balls of your feet. Contract your abs and keep your hips level with your back. Keep your neck long by looking past your hands. Start out holding for 5 slow breaths and add 1 breath every workout until you can do 15.

The Squeeze Factor

The squeeze is the drawing in of the abdominals the entire time. Pull up while keeping your back long and shoulders down.

The Breath Factor

As you inhale, focus on pressing your shoulders down your back and keeping your hips in line with your shoulders and ankles.

As you exhale, focus on pulling your abs up and the obliques (the muscles of your waistline) in.

A Word from Wini

The plank is a stabilization exercise. The muscles are certainly working, yet there is no obvious movement involved.

Focus on having your entire body work together as one unit. Imagine an energy

One Size Does Not Fit All

BEGINNER

To make the exercise easier, try it on your forearms and knees instead of with straight legs. Be sure to keep a straight line from your shoulders to your knees.

ADVANCED

Once you can hold easily for 15 breaths, do 8 breaths with your right leg lifted up a few inches and then 8 breaths with your left leg lifted up.

stream running in a straight line from your head all the way through your hips to the balls of your feet.

Watch Out For

Make sure your shoulders and elbows are in a straight line. Keep the top of your head reaching long, away from your shoulders, to avoid tension in the neck. Pull your shoulders down to avoid hunching them.

Back Extension

STARTING POSITION

Lie facedown on a mat. Interlace your fingers on
your lower back. Your chin is on the floor.

MOVEMENT

Keeping your legs down, draw your glutes and
lower-back muscles in as you raise your chest a few
inches off the floor. Pause for 2 counts. Lower
slowly. Repeat for 10 reps and add 1 rep with each
workout until you can do 15.

The Squeeze Factor

Squeeze your glutes together
and the two columns of your
lower back toward each other as
you come up.

The Breath Factor

Exhale as you lift your chest off
the floor to extend your back.
Inhale as you lower slowly.

A Word from Wini

When first practicing this exercise, put one hand palm down
on your lower back and feel the
two columns of muscle along
your lower back working.
Imagine your back doing a
crunch as your glutes come
together.

One Size Does Not Fit All

BEGINNER

Try this as a static contraction to get familiar with the movement. Bring yourself up and hold for 3 breaths, then release.

ADVANCED

Place your hands behind your head, as shown, to increase the challenge.

"Start from where you are. It is the only place you can."

Watch Out For

Don't come up too high. Focus on reaching your spine longer toward the wall instead of up toward the ceiling. Also remember that your shoulders should stay rolled back at all times.

Lengthening Stretch: Cat Stretch

STARTING POSITION

Start on your hands and knees. Make sure that your hands are directly under your shoulders and your knees are in line with your hips.

THE STRETCH

Part one: Take a deep breath. As you exhale, draw your navel into your spine and round your back by tucking your pelvis under and dropping your head.

The Breath Factor

As you exhale, focus on tucking your tailbone under and relaxing your head. As you inhale, focus on extending your spine and really tipping the pelvis.

A Word from Wini

Try to breathe into your entire lower back as you go through this stretch. Imagine your pelvis as a bowl. As you arch your back, let it tip forward to spill water.

One Size Does Not Fit All

BEGINNER

If this stretch bothers your back, try making the movement smaller by simply tucking your pelvis and releasing.

Part two: Inhale and arch your back and lift your head to look up. Repeat for 5 breaths.

Lengthening Stretch: Child's Pose

STARTING POSITION

Start on your hands and knees with the front of your feet flat on the mat. Make sure that your hands are under your shoulders and your knees are in line with your hips.

THE STRETCH

Drop your hips back so that your glutes are resting on your heels and your chest is resting on your thighs. Bring your forehead to the mat and reach your arms forward. Relax here for 5 full breaths.

One Size Does Not Fit All

BEGINNER

If your glutes don't touch your heels, place a rolled-up towel between your hips and your heels.

The Breath Factor
Breathe deeply and evenly. Relax into the stretch.

A Word from Wini
See if you can really let go in this stretch. Focus on sending your breath to the parts of your body that feel tight. Let the floor totally support you.

Working Out with a Physioroll

Although I've used a Swiss ball in the photos throughout this book, if you're a beginner, you might want to opt for a physioroll instead. Physiorolls are larger than Swiss balls and look like two balls molded together. Their unique peanutlike shape makes them more stable than traditional exercise balls. While a Swiss ball rolls forward and backward as well as side to side, a physioroll rolls only forward and backward. Or, if you lie on it the long way, it rolls only side to side instead of forward and backward.

You can use the physioroll in a variety of ways, depending on the exercise you're doing. For sitting exercises, sit on the ball as if it were a saddle. For abdominal exercises, lie across it with the wider part supporting your back (see photo a). For exercises where you lie on your stomach, such as kickbacks on the ball, lie down lengthwise (b). Finally, for exercises where you lie on your back, such as dumbbell presses on the ball, lie down with the wider part supporting your back if you're just starting out. As you get more comfortable, try lying down lengthwise so you can get a greater range of motion (c).

You can purchase a physioroll at many sporting goods stores. Or type "physioroll" in your favorite search engine to find online sellers. Choose a 70-centimeter physioroll if you're over 6 feet tall. If you're shorter than that, go with one that's 55 centimeters.

a

b

c

Core Basics at a Glance

Each synergy set is designed as a circuit. Do all the exercises or a suggested variation in order with a short rest of 30 to 60 seconds after the entire synergy set is completed. Then repeat for one more complete round before moving on to the next synergy set. By combining the exercises in this way, you'll get a balanced workout that integrates the best strengthening and stretching exercises to keep you lean, long, and strong.

To help track your progress, rewrite or photocopy the Core Basics Training Log on the opposite page. Then simply fill in the number of reps or breaths of each exercise that you complete. That way, the next time you do this workout, you'll know what you'll have to do to keep progressing. (If you prefer to keep your training logs in a binder, you can find versions of the logs without the photos beginning on page 286.)

SYNERGY SET 1

Ball Towel Crunch:
10–25 reps

Diagonal Ball Crunch:
10–25 reps on each side

Hangover Break:
5 breaths

Drape and Stretch:
5 breaths

Core Basics Training Log

Date _____

Synergy Set 1	Reps/Breaths	Round 1	Round 2
Ball Towel Crunch	10–25 reps		
Diagonal Ball Crunch	10–25 reps each side		
Hangover Break	5 breaths		
Drape and Stretch	5 breaths		
Synergy Set 2			
Plank	5–15 breaths		
Back Extension	10–15 reps		
Cat Stretch	5 breaths		
Child's Pose	5 breaths		

SYNERGY SET 2

Plank: 5–15 breaths

Back Extension: 10–15 reps

Cat Stretch: 5 breaths

Child's Pose: 5 breaths

Core Intermediate

The next level after Core Basics, the Core Intermediate workout hits all aspects of your midsection by using an exercise ball, a mat, and a towel. This 10-minute routine integrates strengthening and stretching to give you a balanced workout.

Triple-Count Crunch

STARTING POSITION

Sit upright on an exercise ball. Place a rolled-up towel between your knees. Walk your feet forward, letting the ball roll up your back until it's supporting your lower back. Your knees are in line with your ankles, and your feet are firmly on the floor. Head and shoulders are off the ball. Place your hands behind your head.

MOVEMENT

As you bring your inner thighs together to hug the towel, draw your abs down. Lift your head and shoulders so that your rib cage moves closer to your hips. Press up in 3 counts, contracting your abs a bit more with each count. Lower slowly. Repeat for 10 perfect reps and add 1 rep each workout until you can do 15.

The Squeeze Factor

For each count, keep squeezing your abs down by decreasing the space between your ribs and your hips.

The Breath Factor

Exhale as you bring your ribs closer to your hips. Inhale as you lower yourself back on the ball.

A Word from Wini

Think of increasing the intensity as slowly turning a dial. With each count up, turn up the intensity a little more.

One Size Does Not Fit All

BEGINNER

If you find it difficult to balance on the ball, forget about the towel for now and widen your knees and drop your hips closer to the floor to increase stability.

ADVANCED

Wrap your arms and interlock your hands so that your head is resting on your arms.

Watch Out For

Try not to pull with your head. Imagine being drawn forward by cords on your rib cage that are pulling your ribs closer to your hips.

Side Crunch on Ball

STARTING POSITION

Lie sideways on the exercise ball so that the ball is supporting your right side. Place your left foot in front of your right leg to have a wide base of support. Hands are behind your head.

MOVEMENT

Draw your abs in and press your waist down as you raise your head and shoulders to bring your left ribs closer to your left hip. Pause for a moment and lower slowly. Repeat for 10 perfect reps and then change sides. Start out with 10 reps on each side and add 1 rep with each workout until you can do 25.

The Squeeze Factor

As you do the side crunch, really squeeze the side of your waist in and down as you keep your abs drawn.

The Breath Factor

Exhale as you bring your torso up. Inhale as you lower yourself back on the ball.

A Word from Wini

The first priority is to keep the side of your body in one even line. If you could be seen from the ceiling, only one hip, one side of your rib cage, and one elbow should be visible.

One Size Does Not Fit All

BEGINNER

If you find it difficult to balance on the ball, press your feet against a wall.

ADVANCED

Increase the challenge by increasing the lever. Hold on to a towel and stretch out both arms in line with your ears.

Watch Out For

No big movements here. More important than the size of the movement is the quality of the rep. Keep the movement small and make sure you are pressing down and in as you crunch up.

Lengthening Stretch: Hangover to the Side

STARTING POSITION

Sit on the exercise ball with your feet firmly placed on the floor.

THE STRETCH

Hang forward over the ball and rock forward and back, feeling the stretch in your spine. Walk both hands over to the outside of your right foot, as shown. Hold for 5 slow breaths. Switch sides.

The Breath Factor

As you inhale, lengthen your back by reaching from the top of your head through your tailbone. As you exhale, focus on relaxing your back, feeling the stretch along your side.

A Word from Wini

See if you can really focus on the side being stretched. Notice if one side feels tighter than the other. Try to send your breath into the tighter areas.

Watch Out For

Make sure both hips stay pressed firmly into the ball when you walk your hands to either foot.

One Size Does Not Fit All

BEGINNER

While hanging over the ball, keep your hands on either side of your foot and gently move your torso slightly to one side for 5 breaths. Switch sides.

ALTERNATE EXERCISE

If this stretch is uncomfortable for you, try the Hangover Break (see page 30), as shown.

"When you stretch yourself,
you find out how strong you are."

Plank on Ball

STARTING POSITION

Lie with your abs on the ball and your hands firmly on the floor. Make sure your arms are shoulder-distance apart. Pull your body into a straight line and walk your hands forward until your shins are on the ball.

HOLD POSITION

Keep your body in a straight line from the shoulders through the heels. Roll your shoulders down your back and keep your hands in line with your shoulders. Keep your neck extended and look past your hands. Hold for 5 slow breaths and add 1 breath each workout until you can do 10.

The Squeeze Factor

Draw your abs in and up the entire time. Tighten all the muscles that surround your waist and pull them in like a tight, thick belt.

The Breath Factor

As you inhale, focus on creating a straight line through your body. As you exhale, draw your abs in a little more.

A Word from Wini

The Plank on Ball, like the Plank in the Core Basics workout, is a stabilization exercise. The muscles are certainly working, yet there is no obvious movement involved. The priority here is to keep your body in a straight line, like a plank of wood.

One Size Does Not Fit All

BEGINNER

The closer the ball is to your center, the easier this exercise will be. Try it at first with your thighs supported on the ball.

ADVANCED

Walk your hands farther away so that you can press the balls of your feet into the ball.

Watch Out For

Be careful not to arch your back or drop your hips. There should be no hinging at the waist, just a straight line from your shoulders through your hips.

Hyperextension on Ball

STARTING POSITION

Drape yourself over the ball facedown with your knees relaxed. Press your feet into a wall for support. Hands are behind your head with the elbows open.

MOVEMENT

Draw your navel in and raise your torso from your hips as one unit until your knees and shoulders form a diagonal line with the floor. Repeat for 10 reps and add 1 rep with each workout until you can do 15.

The Squeeze Factor

As you raise your body up, squeeze the columns of your lower back in toward each other while you squeeze the muscles of your glutes up and in.

The Breath Factor

Exhale as you raise your torso up. Inhale as you lower your torso back to the ball.

A Word from Wini

Make sure you're pivoting at the hips and not the waist. Increase your length with every rep by reaching up and out.

One Size Does Not Fit All

BEGINNER

To make the exercise easier, keep your arms at your sides.

ADVANCED

To increase the challenge, extend your arms out in line with your ears.

Watch Out For

Make sure your knees are relaxed. If you find they are hyperextending, press your feet firmly into the wall and bend your knees a little more.

Lengthening Stretch: Drape and Stretch

STARTING POSITION

Kneel with the ball in front of you. Roll forward until the ball supports your midsection. Relax your hands and feet on the floor.

THE STRETCH

Gently rock back and forth over the ball until you find a comfortable position. Hold for 5 slow breaths.

The Breath Factor

As you inhale, focus on increasing the space between your upper chest and lower back. As you exhale, let your body go deeper into the stretch by dropping your head and legs closer to the floor.

A Word from Wini

Find a position where you feel a nice stretch across your lower back. As the workouts pile up, experiment with having the ball higher toward your ribs or lower toward your hips. This is also a great stretch to do after a long day.

Lengthening Stretch: Knees to Chest

STARTING POSITION

Lie on a mat with your neck and shoulders down and relaxed. Bend your knees, lift your legs up, and place your hands on the backs of your thighs.

THE STRETCH

Gently draw in your knees. As you inhale, lengthen your spine. As you exhale, go deeper into the stretch. Hold for 5 slow breaths.

The Breath Factor

As you inhale, focus on lengthening your back on the mat. As you exhale, focus on drawing your knees deeper into your chest.

A Word from Wini

Take the time to breathe into the parts of your body that need it most. Sometimes it is the lower back. Sometimes it's the neck and shoulders. Learn to listen to your body.

Watch Out For

Be careful not to pull your knees in forcefully. Be patient and let your body go where it needs to.

Lengthening Stretch: Knees to Side

STARTING POSITION

Lie on a mat with your neck and shoulders down and relaxed. Extend both arms out in line with your shoulders. Bend your knees to create a 90-degree angle.

THE STRETCH

Gently bring both knees to one side. Turn your head away from your knees. Hold for 5 slow breaths. Switch sides.

The Breath Factor

As you inhale, lengthen your spine by reaching from the top of your head to your tailbone. As you exhale, go deeper into the stretch by letting both shoulders sink into the mat.

A Word from Wini

If you can't breathe comfortably, the stretch is too deep. Find your edge, the place where it is comfortably uncomfortable, and stay there.

Watch Out For

Keep your head and shoulders on the mat.

One Size Does Not Fit All

BEGINNER

For an easier stretch, try placing your knees farther away from your hips.

"Discipline is a muscle, just like the muscles we strengthen in our training. We build it one workout at a time."

Core Intermediate at a Glance

Each synergy set is designed as a circuit. Do all the exercises or a suggested variation in order with a short rest of 30 to 60 seconds coming after the entire synergy set is completed. Then repeat for one more complete round before moving on to the next synergy set. By combining the exercises in this way, you'll get a balanced workout that integrates the best strengthening and stretching exercises to keep you lean, long, and strong.

To help track your progress, rewrite or photocopy the Core Intermediate Training Log on the opposite page. Then simply fill in the number of reps or breaths of each exercise that you complete. That way, the next time you do this workout, you'll know what you'll have to do to keep progressing. (If you prefer to keep your training logs in a binder, you can find versions of the logs without the photos beginning on page 286.)

SYNERGY SET 1

Triple-Count Crunch:
10–15 reps

Side Crunch on Ball:
10–25 reps on each side

Hangover to the Side:
5 breaths on each side

Core Intermediate Training Log

Date _____

Synergy Set 1	Reps/Breaths	Round 1	Round 2
Triple-Count Crunch	10–15 reps		
Side Crunch on Ball	10–25 reps each side		
Hangover to the Side	5 breaths each side		
Synergy Set 2			
Plank on Ball	5–10 breaths		
Hyperextension on Ball	10–15 reps		
Drape and Stretch	5 breaths		
Knees to Chest	5 breaths		
Knees to Side	5 breaths each side		

SYNERGY SET 2

Plank on Ball:
5–10 breaths

Hyperextension on
Ball: 10–15 reps

Drape and Stretch:
5 breaths

Knees to Chest:
5 breaths

Knees to Side:
5 breaths on each side

Core Challenge

The Core Challenge routine builds upon the other routines for defining the core. The exercises flow in a logical sequence, so this routine should take no longer than 12 minutes. All you need for this routine are an exercise ball, a towel, and a mat.

Diagonal Crunch with Leg Lift

STARTING POSITION

Sit upright on an exercise ball. Walk your feet forward, letting the ball roll up your back until it is supporting your mid- and lower back. Head and shoulders are off the ball. Feet are hip-width apart and firmly on the floor. Ankles are in line with your knees. Hands are placed behind your head with the elbows open.

MOVEMENT

Contract your abdominals by bringing your ribs toward your hips. Simultaneously bring your left shoulder toward your right knee and your right knee toward your chest. Pause at the top of the movement for 2 counts. Switch sides. Start out with 10 perfect reps, alternating each side, and add 1 rep per workout until you can do 15.

The Squeeze Factor

As you move diagonally, imagine a sponge between the side you are moving from and your opposite hip. Flatten it first, then wring out the excess water.

The Breath Factor

Exhale as you bring your shoulder toward your knee. Inhale as you lower your shoulder and knee back down.

A Word from Wini

Really press your lower back in toward the ball as you move diagonally. This will help you stay steady on the ball.

One Size Does Not Fit All

BEGINNER

To make the exercise easier, just do the diagonal crunch keeping your feet firmly on the floor.

ADVANCED

Extend one arm out in line with your ear, as shown. By lengthening the lever of your arm, you increase the challenge.

Watch Out For

Stay steady. If you find yourself losing your balance, drop your hips closer to the floor.

Roll-In

STARTING POSITION

Get into a pushup position by lying
prone on an exercise ball. Walk your
hands forward until your thighs are
on the ball. Hands are pressed firmly
on the floor and placed slightly wider
than your shoulders. Your body
should form a straight line from your
heels to the top of your head. Draw
your shoulder blades down into your
back. Keep your neck long by looking
past your hands.

MOVEMENT

Tighten your abs and raise your hips to
an inverted V position. The ball will roll
down your legs toward your shins. Hold
your hips up for 2 counts, then slowly
lower your hips and roll the ball back on
your thighs until your body is in a
straight line again. Start out with 10 reps
and add 1 rep with each workout until
you can do 15 perfect reps.

The Squeeze Factor

Start squeezing your abs up and
in before you even start
moving. As you lift your hips,
visualize all sides of your abs
coming together to meet behind
your belly button.

The Breath Factor

Exhale as you lift your hips up
to form an inverted V. Inhale as
you come back to form a
straight line.

A Word from Wini

Keep the movement small and
controlled. Tuck your pelvis
under and really draw your
belly button down as you roll in.

One Size Does Not Fit All

BEGINNER

Practice just holding the starting position and contracting your abs for a few breaths.

ADVANCED

From the prone position, walk your hands forward until only your feet are on the ball, as shown (top photo). Flexing your feet on the ball, tighten your abs and raise your hips to an inverted V position (bottom photo). Hold for 2 counts, then slowly lower.

Watch Out For

Check to make sure your hands are in line with your shoulders. At the end of every rep, you should be back to a perfect pushup position.

Lengthening Stretch: Super Side Stretch

STARTING POSITION

Kneel with the ball in front of you. Roll forward until the ball supports your midsection. Relax your hands and feet on the floor.

THE STRETCH

Gently rock back and forth over the ball until you find a comfortable position. Place one hand on the floor directly under your shoulder and slightly twist your torso toward the ceiling. Extend one arm in line with your ear to the wall in front of you. Hold for 5 slow breaths. Switch sides.

The Breath Factor

As you inhale, focus on increasing the space between your hips and your shoulders. As you exhale, let your body go deeper into the stretch by reaching your extended arm toward the wall.

A Word from Wini

Find a position where you feel a nice stretch across your side. Really reach out from your feet all the way to the tips of your fingers, creating a straight energy stream.

One Size Does Not Fit All

ALTERNATE EXERCISE

Reach your extended arm toward the ceiling. Reach
the top of your head toward the wall in front of you.

"The harder you work, the less complicated it gets."

Windshield Wiper

STARTING POSITION

Lie on your back and lift your legs toward
the ceiling so they are in line with your hips.
Place a towel between your thighs and
bend your knees, creating a 90-degree
angle. Extend your arms out to the sides in
line with your shoulders.

MOVEMENT

As you draw your inner thighs together to hug
the towel, draw your navel into your spine.
Keeping your abs tight, slowly lower your
legs to one side, gently connecting to
the floor. Return to the center.
Lower your legs to the other
side. Start out with 10 perfect
reps on each side and add
1 rep with each workout
until you can do 15.

The Squeeze Factor

Squeeze the sides of your waist
into your center constantly
throughout the movement.
Think about tightening a thick
belt around your waist from the
inside.

The Breath Factor

Inhale as you lower your legs
from the center to the side. Exhale as you lift your legs off the
floor to return to center.

A Word from Wini

Try to keep your knees in line
with your hips instead of letting
them drop in toward your
chest. Think of your knees as
the hour hand on a clock. They
start at 12 o'clock and go
directly to 3 o'clock, back up
to 12, and over to 9 o'clock.

One Size Does Not Fit All

BEGINNER

Bend your knees closer in
toward your chest.

ADVANCED

Straighten your legs to increase the
lever.

Watch Out For

Make sure your head and shoulders stay connected to the floor.

Superwoman

STARTING POSITION

Lie facedown on a mat. Extend your arms straight out in front of you and extend your legs straight behind you. Extend your neck with your eyes toward the floor.

MOVEMENT

Simultaneously extend your head, shoulders, arms, and legs up and out a few inches off the floor. Pause for 2 counts. Lower slowly. Repeat for 10 reps and add 1 rep with each workout until you can do 15.

The Squeeze Factor

Squeeze your glutes together and the two columns of your lower back in as you come up.

The Breath Factor

Exhale as you raise your arms and legs up. Inhale as you lower your arms and legs.

A Word from Wini

This exercise is harder than it looks. Try to truly reach out instead of up. Visualize creating length in your body as you lift.

One Size Does Not Fit All

BEGINNER

Keep your arms at your sides, as shown.

ADVANCED

Increase the length of the pause at the top to 4 counts.

"Strength is found outside the comfort zone."

Watch Out For

Be careful not to hunch. Keep your neck long by pressing your shoulders down and reaching the top of your head to the wall in front of you.

Figure 4 Crunch

STARTING POSITION

Lie on your back and bend both knees. Place your left ankle over your right thigh. Raise your right foot a few inches off the floor. Place your hands behind your head. Draw your abdominals down.

MOVEMENT

Simultaneously curl both your ribs and hips in toward your center. Pause and hold for 2 counts. Lower slowly and repeat. Do 10 perfect reps, and then switch legs.

The Squeeze Factor

As you bring your ribs and hips toward each other, squeeze your abdominals into the floor beneath you.

The Breath Factor

Exhale as you bring your ribs and hips toward your center. Inhale as you lower them back to starting position.

A Word from Wini

The leg that is crossed over adds some resistance, giving you a built-in abdominal machine within your own body. Really pause and pull down the abs at the top of each rep.

One Size Does Not Fit All

BEGINNER

If this is too challenging, try the Double Crunch (see page 84), but without the towel.

ADVANCED

Increase the lever by extending one hand behind your head in line with your ear.

Watch Out For

The movement is initiated by the abdominals. with the head and shoulders and legs simply going along for the ride. Don't pull with your legs or head; move from your ribs and hips.

Lengthening Stretch: Figure 4 Stretch

STARTING POSITION

Lie on your back and bend both knees. Place your right ankle over your left thigh.

THE STRETCH

Lace your hands under your left thigh. Gently draw in your knees. As you inhale, lengthen your spine. As you exhale, go deeper into the stretch. Hold for 5 slow breaths. Switch legs.

One Size Does Not Fit All

BEGINNER

If this is too difficult, try the Knees to Chest stretch (see page 55).

The Breath Factor

As you inhale, focus on lengthening your back by increasing the space between your upper chest and your lower back. As you exhale, draw your legs closer to your chest.

A Word from Wini

One side can often be much tighter than the other. Hold for a few extra breaths on the side that is tighter. The side you don't want to do is the side you need to do.

Lengthening Stretch: Lying Eagle

STARTING POSITION

Lie on your back with your arms out to the sides in line with your shoulders. Hook your right leg over your left thigh.

THE STRETCH

Keeping your right leg hooked around your left thigh, gently bring your legs over to the left. Turn your head to face the right. Hold for 5 slow breaths. Switch sides.

One Size Does Not Fit All

For an alternative, try the Knees to Side stretch (see page 56).

The Breath Factor

As you inhale, focus on lengthening your body. Visualize breathing into the space between your upper chest and your lower back. As you exhale, go deeper into the gentle twist.

A Word from Wini

Take your time and try to keep your inhaling and exhaling even.

Core Challenge at a Glance

Each synergy set is designed as a circuit. Do all the exercises or a suggested variation in order with a short rest of 30 to 60 seconds after the entire synergy set is completed. Then repeat for one more complete round before moving on to the next synergy set. By combining the exercises in this way, you'll get a balanced workout that integrates the best strengthening and stretching exercises to keep you lean, long, and strong.

To help track your progress, rewrite or photocopy the Core Challenge Training Log on the opposite page. Then simply fill in the number of reps or breaths of each exercise that you complete. That way, the next time you do this workout, you'll know what you'll have to do to keep progressing. (If you prefer to keep your training logs in a binder, you can find versions of the logs without the photos beginning on page 286.)

SYNERGY SET 1

Diagonal Crunch with
Leg Lift: 10–15 reps

Roll-In:
10–15 reps

Super Side Stretch:
5 breaths on each side

Core Challenge Training Log

Date _____

Synergy Set 1	Reps/Breaths	Round 1	Round 2
Diagonal Crunch with Leg Lift	10–15 reps		
Roll-In	10–15 reps		
Super Side Stretch	5 breaths each side		
Synergy Set 2			
Windshield Wiper	10–15 reps each side		
Superwoman	10–15 reps		
Figure 4 Crunch	10 reps each side		
Figure 4 Stretch	5 breaths each side		
Lying Eagle	5 breaths each side		

SYNERGY SET 2

Windshield Wiper:
10–15 reps on each side

Superwoman:
10–15 reps

Figure 4 Crunch:
10 reps on each side

Figure 4 Stretch:
5 breaths on each side

Lying Eagle:
5 breaths on each side

Core Express

Core Express is the routine to do when you want a quick workout that requires just two towels and a mat. This is a balanced routine that easily integrates strengthening and stretching and can be done in 5 minutes.

Towel Crunch

STARTING POSITION

Lie on your back on a mat and place a thick, rolled-up towel beneath your lower back. Place another towel between your inner thighs, and place your feet on the floor. Place your hands behind your head.

MOVEMENT

Contract your abdominals by bringing your rib cage forward and your head and shoulder blades off the mat. Pause and hold for 2 counts. Lower slowly and repeat. Start out with 10 perfect reps and add 1 rep with each workout until you can do 20.

The Squeeze Factor

As you bring your ribs toward your hips, squeeze your abdominals down into your spine. Imagine a string attached to the floor, pulling your belly button all the way down to meet your back.

The Breath Factor

Exhale as you bring your ribs closer to your hips. Inhale as you lower your shoulders back to the mat.

A Word from Wini

The towel under the back ensures that the abdominals are working in a full range of motion. It places your abs in a slightly stretched position just like the exercise ball does.

One Size Does Not Fit All

BEGINNER

Try just a few reps, and place one hand on your abs to really feel the muscle working.

ADVANCED

Increase the challenge by extending one arm in line with your ear, as shown.

Watch Out For

Make sure you are pulling with your abdominals and not your neck and arms. Start the movement with your rib cage moving forward to meet your hips.

Circle Crunch

STARTING POSITION

Lie on your back and place a thick, rolled-up towel beneath your lower back. Place another towel between your knees, and place your feet on the floor. Place your hands behind your head.

MOVEMENT

Exhale and contract your abdominals, bringing your rib cage forward and your head and shoulder blades off the mat. From that position, draw a circle with your ribs toward the right for 10 reps. Repeat toward the left for 10 reps. Add 1 rep in each direction with each workout until you can do 15.

The Squeeze Factor

Draw your abs down to the floor as you begin the circle. As you come to the highest point of the circle, really squeeze the area between your ribs.

The Breath Factor

Exhale as you begin the circle. Inhale as you return to the mat.

A Word from Wini

Really work on drawing a perfect circle with your ribs while at the same time scooping your abs down.

One Size Does Not Fit All

BEGINNER

Try just a few reps in each direction until you develop more core strength.

ADVANCED

Increase the challenge by extending one arm out in line with your ear, as shown.

"Let the workouts pile up. They become the solid ground beneath your feet."

Watch Out For

Be careful not to tug with your head. Draw the circle with your ribs and not your head.

Double Crunch

STARTING POSITION

Lie on your back with your
knees bent. Place a rolled-up
towel between your thighs.
Raise your legs up to a
90-degree angle. Draw your
abdominals in as you hug the
towel with your legs.

MOVEMENT

Raise your head and shoulders and bring your
ribs and hips together by pressing your rib
cage down and tucking your pelvis under.
Pause at the top of the movement and gently
grip the towel as you draw your abs down
even more for 2 counts. Lower slowly and repeat. Start out with 10 perfect reps and add 1
rep with each workout until you can do 20.

The Squeeze Factor
As you pull your ribs and hips
together, draw your abs down
and squeeze. Use the towel to
really connect to the entire
length of the abdominals.

The Breath Factor
Exhale as you draw your ribs
and hips together. Inhale as you
lower your shoulders and hips
back to the mat.

A Word from Wini
Imagine there are magnets between your ribs and your hips,
pulling them close together.

One Size Does Not Fit All

BEGINNER

If this is too challenging, try the Towel Crunch (see page 80).

ADVANCED

Extend your legs a bit past the 90-degree angle, being sure to keep your back on the floor.

Watch Out For

The most common mistake people make when doing reverse crunches is pulling from their knees and neck. Let the movement initiate from where the muscle starts—the ribs, sternum, and hips.

Alternate Arms and Legs

STARTING POSITION

Support your body on your hands and knees. Draw
your shoulder blades down your back and together.
Draw your navel into your spine. Extend your neck
and look at a spot on the floor slightly ahead of you.

MOVEMENT

Lift your right arm and left leg to the level of your
torso. Pause at the top of the movement, keeping
your arm and leg reaching as long as possible.
Lower slowly and repeat for 5 reps. Then switch to
the left arm and right leg for 5 reps. Add 1 rep for
each side per workout until you can do 10.

The Squeeze Factor

As you raise your arm and leg,
squeeze your glutes and mid-
back. Squeeze the glutes up and
together in toward your back.

The Breath Factor

Exhale as you lift your leg and
arm. Inhale as you return your
leg and arm to the mat.

A Word from Wini

Think length instead of height.
Reach out with your arm and
leg instead of up.

One Size Does Not Fit All

BEGINNER

To make the exercise easier, practice lifting just your arms and then just your legs, as shown. As you get stronger, try a couple with the arm and leg lifted simultaneously.

ADVANCED

At the top of each movement, pause and squeeze for an extra breath.

"Dream high. Yet put the building blocks in place to reach your dreams. If you want to lose 100 pounds, take it a few pounds at a time."

Watch Out For

Make sure your neck is long and your shoulder blades are drawn down your back. Check your balance and make sure your weight is evenly distributed between your knee and arm.

Lengthening Stretch: Downward Dog

STARTING POSITION

Start on all fours, with your hands under your shoulders and knees under your hips.

THE STRETCH

Press yourself back, raising your hips toward the ceiling. Press evenly into your hands and pull your shoulders away from your neck. Relax your head and neck. Hold for 5 relaxed breaths.

One Size Does Not Fit All

BEGINNER

If this is too difficult, try the Cat Stretch (see page 36).

The Breath Factor

Breathe evenly. Inhale for the same length of time as you exhale.

A Word from Wini

Press your weight back into your heels and work on tipping your pelvis and keeping your back long. Use this stretch to relax your back and to stretch out your body after all your core work.

Watch Out For

Relax your neck and let your head hang freely while keeping your shoulders down your back, away from your neck. Check your hands and feet to make sure they're pressing evenly into the mat.

Lengthening Stretch: Wide Child's Pose

STARTING POSITION

Start on your hands and knees, with the fronts of your feet flat on the mat. Place your knees a little wider than your hips, and angle your feet toward each other.

THE STRETCH

Drop your hips back so that your glutes are resting on your heels and your chest is resting inside your thighs. Bring your forehead to the mat and walk your arms forward, placing your hands flat on the floor. Relax here for 5 slow breaths.

One Size Does Not Fit All

BEGINNER

If walking your hands out bothers your shoulders, just wrap them around your legs.

A Word from Wini

Every time you inhale, focus on lengthening your spine by reaching through the top of your head. Every time you exhale, focus on relaxing your back.

Core Express at a Glance

Each synergy set is designed as a circuit. Do all the exercises or a suggested variation in order with a short rest of 30 to 60 seconds coming after the entire synergy set is completed. Then repeat for one more complete round. By combining the exercises in this way, you'll get a balanced workout that integrates the best strengthening and stretching exercises to keep you lean, long, and strong.

To help track your progress, rewrite or photocopy the Core Express Training Log on the opposite page. Then simply fill in the number of reps or breaths of each exercise that you complete. That way, the next time you do this workout, you'll know what you'll have to do to keep progressing. (If you prefer to keep your training logs in a binder, you can find versions of the logs without the photos beginning on page 286.)

SYNERGY SET 1

Towel Crunch:
10–20 reps

Circle Crunch: 10–15
reps in each direction

Double Crunch:
10–20 reps

Core Express Training Log

Date _____

Synergy Set 1	Reps/Breaths	Round 1	Round 2
Towel Crunch	10–20 reps		
Circle Crunch	10–15 reps each direction		
Double Crunch	10–20 reps		
Alternate Arms and Legs	5–10 reps each side		
Downward Dog	5 breaths		
Wide Child's Pose	5 breaths		

Alternate Arms
and Legs: 5–10
reps on each side

Downward Dog:
5 breaths

Wide Child's Pose:
5 breaths

DEFINING THE LOWER BODY

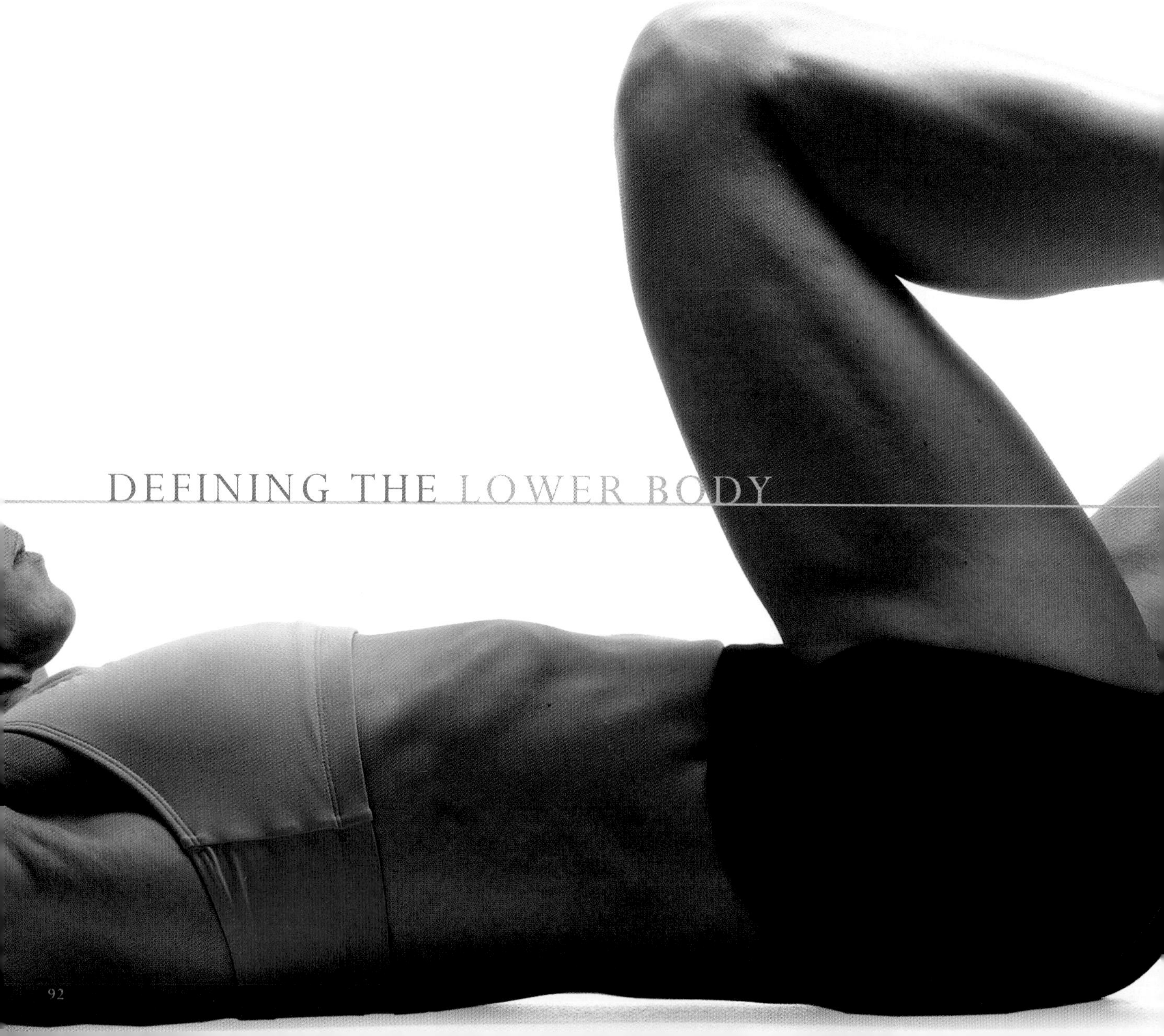

Lower-Body Basics

Lower-Body Basics is an introductory lower-body workout that gets you started working with synergy sets. When first learning the exercises, you just need a mat. As you progress, you'll be adding a set of dumbbells.

Every synergy set integrates a strengthening move and a stretch to provide you with a balanced workout that really works. Once you're familiar with the exercises, this routine should take you no more than 12 minutes.

Wide Squat

STARTING POSITION

Stand tall and place your feet wider than your hips, turning your feet out slightly. Hands are on your waist with your abdominals drawn in. Roll your shoulders back and down.

MOVEMENT

Keeping your knees in line with your ankles, bend your knees until your thighs are parallel to the floor or just above parallel. Pause at the bottom of the movement. Draw your inner thighs together and squeeze your glutes as you lift up. Start out with 10 perfect reps and add 1 rep with each workout until you can do 15.

The Squeeze Factor

At the bottom of the movement, squeeze your inner thighs and glutes together as you move upward. Remember to squeeze *as* you are moving, not just *when* you complete the movement.

The Breath Factor

Inhale as you bend your knees and go down. Exhale as you lengthen your legs to go up.

A Word from Wini

Press evenly into your feet with a little extra emphasis on your instep as you come up to really wake up the inner thighs.

One Size Does Not Fit All

BEGINNER

To start, practice the movement going just halfway down. Work on tightening your glutes and inner thighs as you raise your body up.

ADVANCED

Add a dumbbell. Hold it by the end with your arms placed in front of your body.

Watch Out For

Make sure your knees don't roll inward. If you find this happening, you're probably turning your feet out too much. Just turn your feet to the 11 o'clock and 1 o'clock positions.

Lengthening Stretch: Quarterback Stretch

STARTING POSITION

Take a wide stance with your legs wider than your hips and your feet slightly turned out. Squat down and place your elbows on the insides of your thighs.

THE STRETCH

Press your elbows into your thighs to gently push them open. Drop your hips to slightly above the level of your knees and arch your back. Hold for 5 slow breaths. Place your hands on your knees and come up slowly.

The Breath Factor

As you inhale, lengthen your spine by lifting your head and extending your tailbone back. As you exhale, press deeper into the stretch by gently pressing the insides of your legs outward.

A Word from Wini

Press your shoulders down and back as you drop your hips. This will help increase the stretch.

Watch Out For

Check to make sure your knees are over your toes. If they're rocking inward, decrease the turnout.

One Size Does Not Fit All

BEGINNER

For an easier version, put your hands on your knees and press outward.

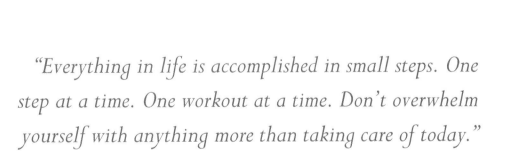

"Everything in life is accomplished in small steps. One step at a time. One workout at a time. Don't overwhelm yourself with anything more than taking care of today."

Drop Lunge

STARTING POSITION

Stand tall and place your feet slightly wider than hip-width apart. Hands are on your waist, and your abdominals are in. Roll your shoulders back and down. Raising your left heel, rotate your whole body to the right, as shown. Make sure your right ankle and knee are in a straight line. Your left heel is up and your right foot is down.

MOVEMENT

Keeping your left heel up, bend your right leg until your thigh is parallel to the floor. Pause at the bottom of the movement. Push your right heel into the floor as you come up. Do 10 reps and then switch sides. Add 1 rep with each workout until you can do 15.

The Squeeze Factor

As you push your heel into the floor to come up, squeeze that glute up and in. Remember to squeeze *as* you are moving, not just when you complete the movement.

The Breath Factor

Inhale as you drop into the lunge. Exhale as you lengthen your legs to come up.

A Word from Wini

Keep your hips even and in line with your shoulders. These are called drop lunges because your hips and torso are dropping *down*, not forward. Imagine that your torso is in a narrow tunnel and can't move forward or back.

One Size Does Not Fit All

BEGINNER

To start, practice the movement going just halfway down.

ADVANCED

Add resistance by holding a dumbbell in each hand.

"Willingness is more essential to start with than willpower."

Watch Out For

Make sure your front knee does not move beyond your ankle.

Lengthening Stretch: Lunge Stretch

STARTING POSITION

Take a wide stance and rotate to the right, floating your left heel up. Your hips are in line with each other, and your right ankle and knee are in a straight line.

THE STRETCH

Bend your right knee and drop both hips toward the floor. Take your hands to either side of your right foot. Gently drop your hips toward the floor, keeping your left leg long. Press out with your left heel. Hold for 5 slow breaths. Switch sides.

The Breath Factor

As you inhale, focus on increasing the space between the top of your head and tailbone. As you exhale, press deeper into the stretch by gently dropping your hips toward the floor.

A Word from Wini

As you press out through your back heel, visualize a long energy stream from your shoulders through your hips to your back foot.

Watch Out For

Make sure your front knee stays in line with your front ankle. Check to make sure both hips are the same height.

One Size Does Not Fit All

BEGINNER

Try putting your hands on your front knee for an easier stretch.

ADVANCED

Place both hands on the floor on the inside of your bent leg and bend your elbows to increase the stretch.

Lying Abduction

STARTING POSITION

Lie on your left side with both legs extended. Your left elbow is bent, and your head is resting on your left hand. Stack your hips so they're directly in line with each other. Stack your shoulders. Press your right hand into the floor directly in front of your ribs to maintain this alignment.
Flex your right foot.

MOVEMENT

Keeping your abs drawn and your torso still, reach your right leg away from you as you lift it up. Pause at the top and then lower the leg slowly.
After 15 perfect reps, switch sides.

One Size Does Not Fit All

BEGINNER

Extend your arm and rest your head on it if this exercise bothers your neck or shoulders.

The Squeeze Factor

At the top of the movement, squeeze the side of the leg up into the glute and squeeze the side of the glute up and in.

The Breath Factor

Exhale as you lift your leg up. Inhale as you lower the leg.

A Word from Wini

This exercise can be as challenging or as easy as you decide it should be. Since it falls after the standing exercises, a few reps will feel like a lot. Work on really extending your leg *away* from your hips as you lift it and on keeping your abs drawn in at all times. See how few you can do until you feel it, not how many.

Watch Out For

Do not rock forward or backward on your hips. Keep your hips in an even line.

Lengthening Stretch: Abductor Stretch

STARTING POSITION

Lie on your back with both legs straight and arms at your sides. Take a moment to make sure both shoulders and hips are evenly placed on the floor.

THE STRETCH

Bring your left knee in until your thigh is perpendicular to the floor. Gently place your right hand on the outside of your left knee. Lightly press your left knee past the midline of your body, keeping it in line with your hip. Hold for 5 slow breaths. Switch sides.

The Breath Factor

As you inhale, lengthen your back on the mat. As you exhale, go deeper into the stretch by gently pressing your thigh across the midline of your body.

A Word from Wini

Imagine your knee is at 12 o'clock. As you press it across the midline of your body, press it 2 hours away: 10 o'clock for the right knee, 2 o'clock for the left. Really focus on the stretch at the side of the thigh all the way up into the glute.

Watch Out For

Make sure your lower back and shoulders stay on the mat.

Lying Adduction

STARTING POSITION

Lie on your left side with both legs extended, your left elbow bent, and your head resting on your left hand. Drop your right knee toward the floor in front of your left leg. Stack your hips so they are directly in line with each other. Press your right hand into the floor directly in front of your ribs to maintain your form. Flex your left foot.

MOVEMENT

Keeping your abs drawn and your torso still, reach your left leg out as you lift it up a few inches. Pause at the top, then lower the leg slowly. After 15 perfect reps, switch sides.

The Squeeze Factor

At the top of the movement, squeeze your inner thigh all the way up into your pelvis.

The Breath Factor

Exhale as you lift your leg up. Inhale as you lower the leg.

A Word from Wini

Floor exercises like the Lying Adduction are often dismissed as too easy. Yet this exercise is an excellent opportunity to understand how the muscles of the inner thigh work. Put your hand on the inside of your

One Size Does Not Fit All

BEGINNER

Extend your arm and rest your head on it if this exercise bothers your neck or shoulders.

"The Lean, Long, and Strong Program works. But it won't work without you. I give you the map. Your job is to get in the car and drive."

thigh and *feel* the muscle lifting up your leg. Instead of seeing how many you can do, try squeezing the inner thigh as hard as you can and seeing how few you can do.

Watch Out For

Don't let your leg turn toward the ceiling. Imagine you have a cup of tea on the inside of your knee.

Lengthening Stretch: Lying Cobbler

STARTING POSITION

Lie on your back with both legs bent and your arms
at your sides. Place your shoulders and hips evenly
on the mat.

THE STRETCH

Bring the soles of your feet together about 2 feet
away from your hips. Let your legs open to the
sides. Draw your tailbone under to lengthen
your back. Hold for 5 slow breaths.

One Size Does Not Fit All

BEGINNER

If this stretch feels too deep or it bothers your lower
back, place a folded towel underneath your hips.

The Breath Factor

As you inhale, reach from the
top of your head through your
tailbone. As you exhale, let
your knees gently drop to the
sides.

A Word from Wini

The secret here is to relax and
breathe. As the workouts pile
up, your flexibility will increase.

Lengthening Stretch: Knees to Chest

STARTING POSITION

From the Lying Cobbler pose, fold your legs together
and draw them in toward your chest. Make sure your
shoulders are evenly placed on the floor.

THE STRETCH

Place your hands on your shins and gently draw
your legs closer to you. Hold for 5 slow breaths. Roll
over on your side and come up slowly.

The Breath Factor

As you inhale, focus on lengthening your back on the mat. As
you exhale, draw your legs in a
little closer.

A Word from Wini

Be patient with the stretch and
stay for the full 5 breaths. Feel
the benefits of each exercise
with this final stretch.

Watch Out For

Avoid pulling your knees in too
forcefully. Keep your head and
shoulders relaxed on the mat.

Lower-Body Basics at a Glance

Each synergy set is designed as a circuit. Do all the exercises or a suggested variation in order with a short rest of 30 to 60 seconds after the entire synergy set is completed. Then repeat for one more complete round before moving on to the next synergy set. By combining the exercises in this way, you'll get a balanced workout that integrates the best strengthening and stretching exercises to keep you lean, long, and strong.

To help track your progress, rewrite or photocopy the Lower-Body Basics Training Log on the opposite page. Then simply fill in the number of reps or breaths of each exercise that you complete. That way, the next time you do this workout, you'll know what you'll have to do to keep progressing. (If you prefer to keep your training logs in a binder, you can find versions of the logs without the photos beginning on page 286.)

SYNERGY SET 1

Wide Squat:
10–15 reps

Quarterback Stretch:
5 breaths

SYNERGY SET 2

Drop Lunge:
10–15 reps on each side

Lunge Stretch:
5 breaths on each side

Lower-Body Basics Training Log

Date _____

Synergy Set 1	Reps/Breaths	Round 1	Round 2
Wide Squat	10–15 reps		
Quarterback Stretch	5 breaths		
Synergy Set 2			
Drop Lunge	10–15 reps each side		
Lunge Stretch	5 breaths each side		
Synergy Set 3			
Lying Abduction	15 reps each side		
Abductor Stretch	5 breaths each side		
Lying Adduction	15 reps each side		
Lying Cobbler	5 breaths		
Knees to Chest	5 breaths		

SYNERGY SET 3

Lying Abduction:
15 reps on each side

Abductor Stretch:
5 breaths on each side

Lying Adduction:
15 reps on each side

Lying Cobbler:
5 breaths

Knees to Chest:
5 breaths

Lower-Body Intermediate

The Lower-Body Intermediate workout is the level-two workout, building upon the Lower-Body Basics workout. When you first learn this workout, you'll need only an exercise ball and a mat. As you progress through the exercises, you will need to add a set of dumbbells.

Every synergy set integrates a strengthening move and a stretch to provide you with a balanced workout that gets your lower body lean, long, and strong. Once you're familiar with the exercises, this routine should take you no more than 12 minutes.

Ball Squat

STARTING POSITION

Place an exercise ball between your lower back and the wall. Stand tall and place your feet wider than your shoulders, with a slight turnout. Walk your feet away from the wall a bit so that you can see them if you glance down. Hands are on your waist, and your abdominals are pulled in. Roll your shoulders back and down.

MOVEMENT

Roll the ball down the wall by bending your knees until your thighs are parallel to the floor or just above parallel. Pause at the bottom of the movement. Draw your inner thighs together and squeeze your glutes as you come up. Repeat for 10 reps. Add 1 rep with each workout until you can do 15.

The Squeeze Factor

As you raise your body up, imagine your glutes are pulling up into the ceiling and your inner thighs are pulling up toward your pelvic floor.

The Breath Factor

Inhale as you bend your knees to come down. Exhale as you squeeze your muscles in to come up.

A Word from Wini

Press your feet evenly and actively into the floor. Notice how much more you can connect to your inner thighs when you press the inside of your foot down.

One Size Does Not Fit All

BEGINNER

Practice the Wide Squat, done without the ball (see page 94).

ADVANCED

Add resistance by holding a dumbbell in each hand.

Watch Out For

Keep your knees in line with your ankles as you come down. If your knees are rocking in, try turning your feet out less.

Lengthening Stretch: Lunge Stretch on Ball

STARTING POSITION

Straddle the ball and then rotate to the right and bend your knees to sit on it. The back of your right thigh and the front of your left hip are on the ball. Your back is long, and your abs are drawn in. Hands are on your waist.

THE STRETCH

Reach out through the top of your head as you gently drop your hips into the ball. Hold for 5 slow breaths. Switch sides.

The Breath Factor

As you inhale, reach from the top of your head through the tip of your tailbone. As you exhale, drop your hips deeper into the ball.

Watch Out For

Be careful not to slump forward. Imagine a string on the top of your head pulling your upper body long. Reach out of your hips and increase the length from your hips to your head.

A Word from Wini

Keep those hips in an even line. Imagine your hips as steady headlights on a car.

One Size Does Not Fit All

BEGINNER

Put your hands on a chair for support.

"Do your workouts. The discipline will build alongside your muscles."

Bridge on Ball

STARTING POSITION

Lie on a mat with the ball under your lower legs. Press your heels firmly on the ball. Your head and neck are relaxed on the mat. Your arms are at your sides, and your abs are drawn in.

MOVEMENT

Lift up your hips until you've formed a diagonal line from your ankles through your hips to your shoulders. Pause at the top for 2 counts, keeping your hips even and steady. Lower slowly until your hips are 2 inches from the floor. Start out with 10 perfect reps and work your way up to 15.

The Squeeze Factor

Squeeze your hamstrings up and in toward your glutes as you raise your hips.

The Breath Factor

Exhale as you lift your hips. Inhale as you lower your hips.

A Word from Wini

Keep your hips even. From the side view, there should be just one hip visible. Imagine two pulleys pulling your hips evenly up toward the ceiling.

One Size Does Not Fit All

BEGINNER

Try a regular bridge without the ball. Lie on a mat with your knees bent and arms at your sides. Feet are parallel to each other and firmly on the floor. Lift your hips up until you've formed a diagonal line from your knees through your hips to your shoulders. Pause at the top for 2 counts, keeping your hips even and steady. Lower slowly until your hips are 2 inches from the floor.

ADVANCED

Do a one-legged bridge with one leg on the ball and one leg pointed straight up toward the ceiling.

Watch Out For

Be careful not to lift too high. Maintain the line from your ankles to your shoulders.

Lengthening Stretch:
Lying Hamstring Stretch with Ball

STARTING POSITION

Lie on your back on a mat and place the ball between your feet and a wall. The ball should be a couple inches off the floor. Move your body as close to the wall as possible. Heels are on the ball.

THE STRETCH

Push your heels into the ball and roll the ball up the wall by straightening your legs. Flex your feet and reach out through your heels. Hold for 5 slow breaths.

The Breath Factor

As you inhale, focus on lengthening your back on the mat from your head through your tailbone. As you exhale, really reach out through your legs all the way into your heels.

A Word from Wini

Really push your heels away from you. Each time you exhale, extend a little more.

Watch Out For

Make sure your hips stay square and on the floor. Check your lower back and make sure you're not arching excessively.

Abduction on Ball

STARTING POSITION

Lie on your left side on an exercise ball with the ball supporting your waist. Extend both legs and put your left hand on the floor. Stack your hips so they're directly in line with each other. Draw in your abs as you lengthen your body over the ball. Press your right hand into the side of your leg, right below your hip. Flex your right foot.

MOVEMENT

Keeping your torso stable, lift your right leg up until it is slightly above the level of your body. Pause at the top for a count of 2 and lower your leg slowly. After 10 reps, switch sides. Add 1 rep with each workout until you can do 15.

One Size Does Not Fit All

BEGINNER

Try the Lying Abduction, done without the ball (see page 102).

The Squeeze Factor

At the top of the movement, squeeze the side of the moving leg all the way up into the glute.

The Breath Factor

Exhale as you lift your leg and squeeze the side of the leg all the way in. Inhale as you lower.

A Word from Wini

Reach *out* before you lift up and see a lean, long leg moving out from the centerline of your body. Think about an energy stream moving from your hip all the way to your heel.

Watch Out For

Make sure you aren't rocking forward or back. Imagine a glass of water balancing on your top hip.

Adduction on Ball

STARTING POSITION

Lie on your right side on an exercise ball with the
ball supporting your waist. Extend both of your legs
and put your right hand on the floor. Stack your hips
so they're directly in line with each other. Draw in
your abs and lengthen your body over the ball. Take
your left leg across the right and rest your left foot
on the floor slightly in front of you. Lengthen and
slightly turn out your right leg. Press your
left hand into the side of your leg right
below your hip. Flex your right foot.

MOVEMENT

Keeping your torso steady, reach out and
up with your right leg. Pause at the top for
a count of 2 and then lower the leg slowly
until it is about 4 inches from the floor.
After 10 perfect reps, switch sides. Start
out with 10 reps on each side and
add 1 rep with each workout
until you can do 15.

The Squeeze Factor

At the top of the movement,
squeeze your inner thigh all the
way up in toward your center.

The Breath Factor

Exhale as you lift your leg and
squeeze the inner thigh inward.
Inhale as you lower your leg.

A Word from Wini

Reach *out* before you lift up by
really reaching through the
heel. See how long you can get
that leg before you even start to
lift it.

One Size Does Not Fit All

BEGINNER

Try the Lying Adduction, done without the ball (see page 104).

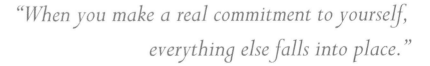

"When you make a real commitment to yourself, everything else falls into place."

Watch Out For

Don't slam your leg down with every rep. Work on staying in the upper half of the movement, or 4 inches above the floor.

Lengthening Stretch: Figure 4 on Ball

STARTING POSITION

Sit on an exercise ball with your spine long and your feet firmly on the floor. Square your hips and draw your abs in.

THE STRETCH

Cross your left ankle across your right thigh and place it above the knee. Lengthen your back and place your left hand on your left knee and your right hand on your left ankle. Gently press your left knee outward. Hold for 5 slow breaths and then switch sides.

The Breath Factor

During the stretch, keep breathing into your hips. As you inhale, make your spine long. Extend from the top of your head through your tailbone. As you exhale, gently press on your legs to increase the stretch.

A Word from Wini

This stretch is a great opportunity to stretch those muscles in the hips. This stretch is challenging and the one most often skipped. Try to notice the exercises you want to skip or rush through. They're usually the ones from which you'll benefit the most.

Watch Out For

Don't force your leg where it doesn't want to go. Sit up tall and just put in the time staying in this stretch. As the workouts pile up, your flexibility will increase.

One Size Does Not Fit All

BEGINNER

Start with a Figure 4 Stretch while lying on a mat (see page 74). Cross your ankle across your thigh and gently draw it in to your chest.

ADVANCED

Lean your torso over your thighs during the stretch and let your head and arms hang toward the floor.

Lower-Body Intermediate at a Glance

Each synergy set is designed as a circuit. Do all the exercises or a suggested variation in order with a short rest of 30 to 60 seconds after the entire synergy set is completed. Then repeat for one more complete round before moving on to the next synergy set. By combining the exercises in this way, you'll get a balanced workout that integrates the best strengthening and stretching exercises to keep you lean, long, and strong.

To help track your progress, rewrite or photocopy the Lower-Body Intermediate Training Log on the opposite page. Then simply fill in the number of reps or breaths of each exercise that you complete. That way, the next time you do this workout, you'll know what you'll have to do to keep progressing. (If you prefer to keep your training logs in a binder, you can find versions of the logs without the photos beginning on page 286.)

SYNERGY SET 1

Ball Squat:
10–15 reps

Lunge Stretch on Ball:
5 breaths on each side

SYNERGY SET 2

Bridge on Ball:
10–15 reps

Lying Hamstring
Stretch with Ball:
5 breaths

Lower-Body Intermediate Training Log

Date _____

Synergy Set 1	Reps/Breaths	Round 1	Round 2
Ball Squat	10–15 reps		
Lunge Stretch on Ball	5 breaths each side		
Synergy Set 2			
Bridge on Ball	10–15 reps		
Lying Hamstring Stretch with Ball	5 breaths		
Synergy Set 3			
Abduction on Ball	10–15 reps each side		
Adduction on Ball	10–15 reps each side		
Figure 4 on Ball	5 breaths each side		

SYNERGY SET 3

Abduction on Ball:
10–15 reps on each
side

Adduction on Ball:
10–15 reps on each
side

Figure 4 on Ball:
5 breaths on each side

Lower-Body Challenge

The Lower-Body Challenge workout builds upon the previous routines for the lower body. The exercises flow in a logical sequence, so this routine should take no longer than 15 minutes. All you need for this routine is a set of weights and a mat. As you progress, you'll add an exercise ball.

Walking Lunge

STARTING POSITION

Stand tall with your hands on your hips. Legs are together with your toes pointing forward. Draw your abdominals in and your shoulders down and back.

MOVEMENT

Take a giant step forward with your right leg by bending your right knee and letting your hips descend. Lower yourself until your left knee is about 3 inches from the floor. Press your right foot firmly into the floor to lift yourself up, then take another giant step forward with your left leg. Repeat for 10 steps. Add 2 steps each workout until you can do 16.

The Squeeze Factor

As you raise your body up, press your front heel down and squeeze your glutes together. Imagine squeezing something between your glutes every time you lift yourself up.

The Breath Factor

Inhale as you take a step forward. Exhale as you press your heel into the floor to come up.

A Word from Wini

When you're learning the exercise, put your hands on your glutes. You'll feel your glute working in your leading leg as you lift yourself up.

One Size Does Not Fit All

BEGINNER

Instead of one giant step right after the other, return to a relaxed stance and pause in between each rep.

ADVANCED

Hold a dumbbell in each hand, with your arms alongside your body, as shown. Increase the weight when you can do 16 steps in good form.

ALTERNATE EXERCISE

If this exercise bothers your knees, try the Drop Lunge instead, as shown (see page 98).

Watch Out For

Make sure the leading leg is bending no more than 90 degrees as you keep your knee in line with your ankle.

Wide Squat with Calf Raise

STARTING POSITION

Stand tall and place your feet slightly wider than your hips, with a slight turnout. Hands are on your waist, with your abdominals drawn in. Roll your shoulders back and down. Keeping your knees in line with your ankles, bend your knees until your thighs are parallel to the floor or just above parallel. Pause at the bottom of the movement and come up onto the balls of your feet.

MOVEMENT

Draw your inner thighs together and squeeze your glutes as you lengthen your legs and come up, staying on the balls of your feet. Lower your heels. Repeat for 10 reps. Add 1 rep each workout until you can do 15.

The Squeeze Factor

At the bottom of the movement, squeeze your inner thighs up and your glutes in as you move upward. Remember to squeeze *as* you are moving, not just when you complete the movement.

The Breath Factor

As you inhale, bend your knees. As you exhale, press the balls of your feet into the floor and come up.

A Word from Wini

Although this is a lower-body challenge movement, it is not just your legs that are benefiting. Your ever-important core is keeping you upright and balanced. Let all the muscles work together to execute a perfect rep.

One Size Does Not Fit All

BEGINNER

If this is too difficult, try doing the Wide Squat without the calf raise (see page 94).

ADVANCED

Increase the intensity by adding a dumbbell. Hold it in front of your body by the end, with your arms long.

Watch Out For

To make sure your feet don't roll out, press extra hard on the big toe side of your feet when you come up onto the balls of your feet.

Lengthening Stretch: Deep Quarterback Stretch

STARTING POSITION

Take a wide stance, with your legs wider than your hips and your feet slightly turned out. Press your hands into the floor as you bend your knees. Draw your abdominals in as you arch your back.

THE STRETCH

Gently press your hips up as you lengthen your legs. Reach up through your hips as your head stays down. Hold for 5 slow breaths. Place your hands on your knees and come up slowly.

The Breath Factor

As you inhale, extend your back by reaching from your tailbone to the top of your head. As you exhale, work on pressing your feet into the floor and reaching through your hips.

A Word from Wini

Visualize your hips reaching up and away from you. Step a little extra onto the instep of your foot to turn on all the lights in your legs.

Watch Out For

Don't lock your knees as you raise your hips up. Keep a soft bend in them at all times.

One Size Does Not Fit All

BEGINNER

For an easier version, try a regular Quarterback Stretch by placing your elbows on the insides of your thighs and gently pressing out (see page 96).

"In each workout, we find out what we can't do. We push ourselves until we cannot do another rep. In finding out what we cannot do, we find out what we can do."

Stiff-Legged Deadlift

STARTING POSITION

Hold a dumbbell in each hand, with arms alongside your body. Legs are shoulder-width apart, and your feet are parallel. Draw your abdominals in and your shoulders down and back.

MOVEMENT

Keeping your back slightly arched, draw your hips back as you tilt forward. Pause when you feel a slight stretch. Come up by pushing your hips forward. Repeat for 15 reps.

The Squeeze Factor

As you raise your body up, squeeze your hamstrings up and in toward your glutes.

The Breath Factor

Inhale as you bend forward and lower the weight. Exhale as you come up and press your hips forward.

A Word from Wini

Remember: The *only* moving joints are your hips. Your hips go back as you pivot forward. Keep the weights very close to the sides of your legs.

One Size Does Not Fit All

BEGINNER

Practice the movement without weights at first, as shown. As you get used to the movement, try a very small range of motion.

ADVANCED

The way to increase the intensity of this exercise is to increase the weight until it is challenging to complete 15 reps.

ALTERNATE EXERCISE

If this exercise bothers your back, do the regular bridge (see page 117), as shown.

Watch Out For

Make sure you aren't rounding your back. Keep your back slightly arched throughout the movement.

Lengthening Stretch: Standing Cross-Legged Bend

STARTING POSITION

Stand tall with your feet hip-width apart. Square your hips and shoulders and draw your abs tight. Cross one leg over the other and press your feet firmly on the floor.

THE STRETCH

Let your hips drift back as your torso comes down and your arms reach toward the floor. Lengthen your spine and relax your head and shoulders. Hold for 5 slow breaths, then come up slowly. Repeat with your legs crossed the opposite way.

The Breath Factor

As you inhale, focus on lengthening your spine. As you exhale, focus on dropping your head and bringing your chest closer to your knees.

A Word from Wini

This stretch is a little gentler on the back than the traditional standing forward bend. Let the pull of gravity on your head and shoulders help you to increase the stretch.

Watch Out For

Make sure both feet are firmly and evenly pressed into the floor.

One Size Does Not Fit All

BEGINNER

If you can't press your hands to the floor, rest them on the tops of your feet or on your knees.

ADVANCED

Place your palms flat on the floor alongside your feet.

One-Legged Bridge

STARTING POSITION

Lie on a mat with your knees bent and arms at your sides. Feet are parallel to each other and firmly on the floor. Straighten your right leg toward the ceiling and flex the foot. Roll your shoulders back and down. Draw your abs in.

MOVEMENT

With your right leg extended up, raise your hips. Lift your hips up until you have a straight line from your left knee through your hips to your shoulders. Pause at the top, contracting your glutes and keeping your navel drawn in. Lower slowly, keeping your foot firmly down. Repeat for 10 reps and switch sides. Add 1 rep each workout until you can do 15.

The Squeeze Factor

Think about pressing the heel into the floor, and squeeze that hamstring up and into the glute.

Remember to squeeze *as* you are moving, not just when you complete the movement.

A Word from Wini

Try to make a perfectly aligned footprint on the ceiling with the extended leg as you lift your hips up.

Watch Out For

Keep your hips level at all times. Do not lift too high. Your hips should always be below the level of your knees.

One Size Does Not Fit All

BEGINNER

Try a bridge with both feet down (see page 117).

ADVANCED

Try the One-Legged Bridge on an exercise ball.

"You are the star of the movie of your life.
You are the writer, director, and casting agent.
Remember, this is your time."

Lengthening Stretch: Lying Stretch and Extend

STARTING POSITION

Lie on your back with both knees bent and arms at
your sides. Take a moment to elongate your neck
and drop your shoulders away from your ears.

THE STRETCH

Bring your right knee in toward your chest. Interlock
your hands around the thigh and pull in gently.
Straighten the leg, as shown, pressing the heel into
the ceiling. Hold for 5 slow breaths. Switch sides.

The Breath Factor

As you inhale, focus on lengthening your back on the mat. As
you exhale, focus on reaching
through the extended leg.

A Word from Wini

As you draw the knee in, focus
on keeping the rest of your
body relaxed. Visualize the
backs of your shoulders and
hips melting into the floor.

Watch Out For

Don't tug the leg in. Be gentle
with yourself. Find your edge,
where you feel a slight stretch,
and breathe into it.

One Size Does Not Fit All

BEGINNER

If you can't interlock your hands behind your thigh, bring them near the top of your knee and gently pull the leg in.

ADVANCED

Extend the leg you aren't stretching flat on the floor.

Lying Side Passé

STARTING POSITION

Lie on your right side with both legs extended and your right arm in line with your right leg. Your right elbow is bent, and your head is resting on your right hand. Stack your hips so they're directly in line with each other. Press your left hand into the floor directly in front of your ribs to maintain your alignment. Keeping your abs drawn in and your torso stable, turn your left leg out and bend the left knee in to connect the toe of the left foot with the inner right thigh.

MOVEMENT

Part one: Extend your left leg toward the ceiling, really reaching out through the toe as you lengthen your leg.

The Squeeze Factor

As you raise the leg up and turn it out, squeeze the outer thigh and glute. As you lower your leg back down, squeeze the inner thigh.

The Breath Factor

Inhale as you extend the leg up to the ceiling. Exhale as you press the leg back down.

A Word from Wini

Think about your leg growing longer with each rep. Reach past the toe into the ceiling. See how few you can do, not how many!

One Size Does Not Fit All

Beginner

Extend your arm and rest your head on it if this exercise bothers your neck or shoulders.

Part two: Lower the leg slowly and repeat for 10 reps.
After 10 perfect reps, switch sides.
Add 1 rep per workout
until you can do 15.

Watch Out For

Don't let your body rock back.
Keep your hips in an even line.
The priority is to keep your
torso and bottom leg absolutely
still.

Side Lift and Circle

STARTING POSITION

Lie on your right side with both legs extended. Your right elbow is bent, and your head is resting on your right hand. Your right elbow, shoulder, hip, and heel are in a straight line. Bend your left leg and place your left foot behind your right knee. Stack your hips so they're directly in line with each other. Press your left hand into the floor directly in front of your ribs to maintain your form.

MOVEMENT

Keeping your abs drawn in and your torso still, reach your right leg away from you as you lift it up a few inches. Reach through your heel as you draw 5 small, controlled circles clockwise. Continue to reach through your heel as you do 5 small controlled circles counterclockwise. Switch sides. Start out with 5 reps in each direction and add 1 rep with each workout until you can do 10.

One Size Does Not Fit All

BEGINNER

Rest your head on your upper arm. Do as many reps as you can and add 1 rep with each workout until you can do 10 in each direction.

The Squeeze Factor

Squeeze the inner thigh of the raised leg all the way up into your center with each lift and circle.

The Breath Factor

Exhale as you begin each circle. Inhale as you complete each circle.

A Word from Wini

Keep reaching through your heel during the entire movement. Reach out before you reach up. Imagine two pulleys on your leg. One is attached to your heel and is drawing your leg long. The other is attached to your inner thigh and is pulling you up with each circle.

Watch Out For

Don't let your leg turn toward the ceiling. Keep that knee facing the wall in front of you.

Lengthening Stretch: Lying Eagle

STARTING POSITION

Lie on your back with your legs extended and your arms out to the sides. Bend your right leg and hook it under your left thigh above the knee.

THE STRETCH

Rotate both legs toward the right, keeping your shoulders down. Hold for 5 slow breaths. For a deeper stretch, turn your head and look toward your left hand. Switch sides.

One Size Does Not Fit All

BEGINNER

Hug your hooked legs toward your chest instead of taking them to the side.

The Breath Factor

As you inhale, focus on lengthening your back on the floor. As you exhale, focus on dropping your legs deeper into the floor.

A Word from Wini

If you can't breathe evenly, you're pushing too hard. Let your breathing be slow and relaxed.

Watch Out For

Keep your shoulders on the floor and your arms long. To avoid hunching your neck, reach out through the top of your head.

Lower-Body Challenge at a Glance

Each synergy set is designed as a circuit. Do all the exercises or a suggested variation in order with a short rest of 30 to 60 seconds after the entire synergy set is completed. Then repeat for one more complete round before moving on to the next synergy set. By combining the exercises in this way, you'll get a balanced workout that integrates the best strengthening and stretching exercises to keep you lean, long, and strong.

To help track your progress, rewrite or photocopy the Lower-Body Challenge Training Log on the opposite page. Then simply fill in the number of reps or breaths of each exercise that you complete. That way, the next time you do this workout, you'll know what you'll have to do to keep progressing. (If you prefer to keep your training logs in a binder, you can find versions of the logs without the photos beginning on page 286.)

SYNERGY SET 1

Walking Lunge: 10–16 steps

Wide Squat with Calf Raise: 10–15 reps

Deep Quarterback Stretch: 5 breaths

Stiff-Legged Deadlift: 15 reps

Standing Cross-Legged Bend: 5 breaths on each side

Lower-Body Challenge Training Log

Date _____

Synergy Set 1	Reps/Breaths	Round 1	Round 2
Walking Lunge	10–16 steps		
Wide Squat with Calf Raise	10–15 reps		
Deep Quarterback Stretch	5 breaths		
Stiff-Legged Deadlift	15 reps		
Standing Cross-Legged Bend	5 breaths each side		
Synergy Set 2			
One-Legged Bridge	10–15 reps each side		
Lying Stretch and Extend	5 breaths each side		
Lying Side Passé	10–15 reps each side		
Side Lift and Circle	5–10 circles each direction, each side		
Lying Eagle	5 breaths each side		

SYNERGY SET 2

One-Legged Bridge: 10–15 reps on each side

Lying Stretch and Extend: 5 breaths on each side

Lying Side Passé: 10–15 reps on each side

Side Lift and Circle: 5–10 circles in each direction on each side

Lying Eagle: 5 breaths on each side

Lower-Body Express

Lower-Body Express is a great workout to do when you are on the road or are pressed for time. It can be done in 8 minutes, and the only equipment you need is a mat.

Around-the-World Squat

STARTING POSITION

Stand tall and place your feet wider than your hips, with a slight turnout. Hands are on your waist with your abdominals drawn in. Roll your shoulders back and down. Keeping your knees in line with your ankles, bend your knees until your thighs are parallel to the floor or slightly above it.

MOVEMENT

Part one: Keeping your knees bent, pull halfway up and then back down for 4 controlled counts. Staying low, rotate to the right, as shown, by floating your left heel up and keeping your right knee bent. Stay here and drop your back knee a little closer to the floor as you squeeze your glutes.

The Squeeze Factor

As you pull up, squeeze the muscles in your legs up and in toward your center. When you pivot to the side, squeeze your glutes together and up.

The Breath Factor

Exhale as you pull up and rotate. Inhale as you press down.

A Word from Wini

Make sure you pivot your whole body when you rotate. The secret is to let the back heel float. Keep your back long by reaching up through the crown of your head.

Part two: Come back to the center and press and pull up again for 4 controlled counts. Staying low, rotate to the left, as shown, by floating your right heel up and keeping your left knee bent. Pause here and drop your back knee a little closer to the floor as you squeeze your glutes. Rotate back to the center and repeat for 2 more cycles.

One Size Does Not Fit All

BEGINNER

Practice the movement without going all the way down, as shown. Practice the rotation and remember to keep your abs tight and torso long.

ADVANCED

Instead of pulling up and down for 4 counts, do so for 8 counts.

Watch Out For

Make sure you start with your legs wide enough so that when you rotate, your knee is in line with your ankle.

Lengthening Stretch: Windmill Stretch

STARTING POSITION

Take a wide stance with your feet slightly turned out. Lift your arms out to the sides in line with your shoulders. Bend your right leg, keeping your knee in line with your toe. Keeping both arms long, windmill your arms so that your left hand is holding the side of your right foot.

THE STRETCH

Keeping your left hand on your right foot, slowly lengthen your right leg. Hold for 5 slow breaths. Come up slowly and switch sides.

The Breath Factor

As you inhale, reach your spine long from your tailbone through the top of your head. As you exhale, go deeper into the rotation.

A Word from Wini

Use the rotation of your opposite hand on the foot to deepen the stretch.

Watch Out For

Make sure you don't hyperextend your knees. Keep a very slight bend when you lengthen.

One Size Does Not Fit All

BEGINNER

If reaching toward your foot is too much, reach toward the outside of your thigh and keep your knees bent.

"The secret is not to forget what you want to accomplish. Decide what you want."

Balance Bend

STARTING POSITION

Stand tall with your hands on your hips. Feet are slightly wider than hip-distance apart, with the toes pointing forward. Draw your abdominals in and your shoulders down and back.

MOVEMENT

Place your arms straight out in front of you, in line with your shoulders. Bend both knees to slowly lower your body a few inches. Hold for 5 slow breaths. Add 1 breath each workout until you can do 15.

The Squeeze Factor

Tighten the back of your hamstrings, feeling the muscles wrap in toward your inner thighs. Squeeze your glutes up and in.

The Breath Factor

As you inhale, focus on reaching the crown of your head toward the ceiling. As you exhale, focus on dropping your hips toward the floor.

A Word from Wini

Imagine you are sitting on a chair. The secret is to let your core strength help you balance and your leg strength keep your body low. Draw those abs in and tighten those glutes.

One Size Does Not Fit All

BEGINNER

If you have trouble balancing, hold on to a chair with one hand.

ADVANCED

Come up onto the balls of your feet before you go down. This is a great balance challenge. Try it for a few breaths before you drop your heels.

Watch Out For

Make sure you aren't going down too low. Double-check that your knees are directly over your toes.

Lengthening Stretch: Standing Forward Bend

STARTING POSITION

Stand with your feet pointing straight ahead, hip-width apart. Knees are soft and relaxed. Square your hips and shoulders and draw your abs tight. Reach your arms up over your head and lengthen your back.

THE STRETCH

Let your hips drift back as your torso comes down and your hands reach toward the floor at the sides of your feet. Lengthen your spine and relax your head and shoulders. Hold for 5 slow breaths.

The Breath Factor

Use your breath to help you. As you inhale, focus on extending the space between the crown of your head and your tailbone. As you exhale, focus on relaxing into the stretch.

A Word from Wini

During the stretch, keep pressing your hips up and away from you while pressing your hands down.

Watch Out For

Make sure your back is long and not rounded. Think about bending over from the hips, not the waist.

One Size Does Not Fit All

BEGINNER

If you can't press your hands to the floor, rest them on the tops of your feet or the fronts of your shins.

ADVANCED

Try to press your palms flat on the floor.

"We cannot wait for a commitment to fitness. We must go out and build it."

Express Leg Circles

STARTING POSITION

Lie on your right side with both legs extended and your head resting on your right hand. Stack your hips so they are directly in line with each other. Press your left hand into the floor directly in front of your ribs to maintain your form. Flex your left foot.

MOVEMENT

Keeping your abs drawn in and your torso still, reach your left leg away from you as you lift it up a few inches. From there, trace a small circle clockwise for 5 reps. Pause in between each rep and reach out through your toes. Keeping your leg up, trace a small circle counterclockwise for 5 reps. Lower the leg slowly. Repeat on the other side. Start out with 5 reps in each direction and add 1 rep with each workout until you can do 10.

One Size Does Not Fit All

BEGINNER

Lengthen your arm and rest your head on it if this exercise bothers your neck or shoulders.

The Squeeze Factor

As you circle the leg, squeeze the entire leg, including the inner thigh, in and upward toward your hip.

The Breath Factor

Exhale as you begin the circle. Inhale as you pause between each circle.

A Word from Wini

This is a super-express exercise! You are working your entire leg as well as your core.

Watch Out For

Be careful not to rock forward and back. Maintain a steady base by keeping your abs drawn in and your hips square.

Lengthening Stretch: One-Legged Stretch and Extend

STARTING POSITION

Start on all fours with your hands underneath your shoulders and your knees underneath your hips. Square your hips and shoulders and draw your abs tight. Lengthen your neck and look at the floor. As you press the heels of your feet into the floor, raise your hips up toward the ceiling.

THE STRETCH

Lengthen your spine and tip your hips up and away from you. Press evenly into your feet and hands. Extend your right leg up and away from you. Point your right toe and lengthen your leg from the hip all the way to the toe. Hold for 5 slow breaths. Place your foot down and switch sides.

One Size Does Not Fit All

BEGINNER

Practice holding just the first part of the stretch with both feet firmly on the floor.

The Breath Factor

As you inhale, focus on lengthening your spine from the top of your head to your tailbone. As you exhale, focus on extending your leg from the hip through the toe.

A Word from Wini

During the stretch, keep reaching out through your hip. Imagine your breath going into all the tight places in your hip. As the workouts add up, your breath will reach a little deeper.

Watch Out For

Press evenly into your hands. If you feel this in your wrist, really focus on pressing your weight back into your legs. To help with your balance, remember to square those hips. Alignment and control will help you stay centered.

Lower-Body Express at a Glance

Each synergy set is designed as a circuit. Do all the exercises or a suggested variation in order with a short rest of 30 to 60 seconds after the entire synergy set is completed. Then repeat for one more complete round before moving on to the next synergy set. By combining the exercises in this way, you'll get a balanced workout that integrates the best strengthening and stretching exercises to keep you lean, long, and strong.

To help track your progress, rewrite or photocopy the Lower-Body Express Training Log on the opposite page. Then simply fill in the number of reps or breaths of each exercise that you complete. That way, the next time you do this workout, you'll know what you'll have to do to keep progressing. (If you prefer to keep your training logs in a binder, you can find versions of the logs without the photos beginning on page 286.)

SYNERGY SET 1

Around-the-World Squat: 3 cycles of 4 reps

Windmill Stretch: 5 breaths on each side

Balance Bend: 5–15 breaths

Standing Forward Bend: 5 breaths

Lower-Body Express Training Log

Date _____

Synergy Set 1	Reps/Breaths	Round 1	Round 2
Around-the-World Squat	3 cycles of 4 reps		
Windmill Stretch	5 breaths each side		
Balance Bend	5–15 breaths		
Standing Forward Bend	5 breaths		
Synergy Set 2			
Express Leg Circles	5–10 reps each direction, each side		
One-Legged Stretch and Extend	5 breaths each side		

SYNERGY SET 2

Express Leg Circles:
5–10 reps in each
direction on each side

One-Legged Stretch
and Extend: 5 breaths
on each side

DEFINING THE UPPER BODY

Upper-Body Basics

Upper-Body Basics is the introductory level of your upper-body workout. All you need are a set of dumbbells, a towel, and a mat. Like all the synergy workouts, this routine integrates stretching and strengthening to provide you with a balanced workout. Once you're familiar with the exercises, this routine can be done in 10 minutes.

Close-Grip Row

STARTING POSITION

Hold a dumbbell in each hand. Align your feet shoulder-width apart, with your knees pointing straight ahead. Hinging at your hips, bend over, keeping your back long by tightening your abs and very slightly arching your lower back. Your torso should be a few inches above parallel to the floor. Keep your knees slightly bent and your back slightly arched to protect it. Draw your abdominals in and draw your shoulders down and back. Your arms are hanging down with the palms turned in.

MOVEMENT

Keeping your palms facing each other, draw your shoulder blades together and bring your elbows up until they move past the level of your back. Pause and draw your arms into your sides and your elbows toward each other. Slowly lower your arms and repeat for 12 perfect reps.

The Squeeze Factor

Start squeezing your upper-back muscles in and together as soon as you initiate the movement. As your elbows come above your back, really work on squeezing your shoulder blades together.

The Breath Factor

Exhale as you lift the weight and inhale as you lower the weight.

One Size Does Not Fit All

BEGINNER

Keep your body a little higher with your head in the 1 o'clock position as viewed from the side, as shown, until you develop enough core strength to bend over more.

ADVANCED

The way to increase the intensity of this exercise is to increase the weight until it is challenging to complete 12 reps.

A Word from Wini

To understand the main muscle you are working, raise your right arm up and take your left arm across your body with your hand underneath your arm. Now pull your right arm down and feel the muscle with your left hand. Say hello to your lats!

Watch Out For

Avoid a slump in your lower back by making sure you're hinging at your hips and not your waist, while maintaining a natural arch in your lower back. Be sure not to bend over too much. Stay slightly above parallel to the floor.

Prep Pushup

STARTING POSITION

Start on all fours on a mat. Place a rolled-up towel in between your thighs. Place your hands a little wider than your shoulders, with your fingers pointing straight ahead and your palms flat down.

MOVEMENT

Part one: Keeping the towel between your thighs, walk your legs out until they are straight, with your toes on the mat. Look down, and keep your head in line with your body.

Your body is now in a straight line from your shoulders through your hips all the way to your ankles. Keep your shoulders down your back and press out through the balls of your feet. Hold this position for 3 slow breaths.

The Squeeze Factor

As you hold the Prep Pushup position, focus on placing your shoulder blades together, drawing your abs in, and squeezing your chest muscles.

The Breath Factor

As you inhale, imagine your breath going directly through the straight line of your body. As you exhale, draw your belly button in and push your hands firmly into the floor.

A Word from Wini

Unlike the traditional "ladies' pushup" done on your knees, this pushup integrates your whole body into the exercise. The towel helps you connect to your core strength, and that will help you hold your form.

Part two: Push yourself back to rest your chest on your knees in the Child's Pose for 3 breaths. Repeat two more times.

One Size Does Not Fit All

BEGINNER

If this is too difficult, start on your knees and hands instead, as shown. Be sure to keep a straight line from your shoulders through your knees.

ADVANCED

Hold for 8 breaths instead of 3.

Watch Out For

Be careful not to sag at the waist or bend at the hips. Priority number one is to keep a straight line from your shoulders to your knees.

Lengthening Stretch: Easy-Open Stretch

STARTING POSITION

From the last Child's Pose after the Prep Pushup, sit back on your heels and sit up tall, as if a string were pulling you toward the ceiling. Lengthen your arms over your head, in line with your ears, with the palms facing in.

THE STRETCH

Slowly bring your arms out to your sides, in line with your shoulders, and turn the palms to face forward. Extend your arms slightly behind you and flex your wrists. Hold for 5 breaths.

The Breath Factor

As you inhale, lengthen your spine from the top of your head through your tailbone. As you exhale, focus on reaching your arms out and back.

A Word from Wini

Extend your arms out to the sides and slightly flex your wrist (point your fingers back) to really work the entire length of your arms. Imagine an energy stream traveling from your shoulders through the center of your palms.

Watch Out For

Don't overarch your back. The stretch is coming from your chest and upper back, not the lower back.

One Size Does Not Fit All

BEGINNER

If it's uncomfortable to sit on your heels, do the stretch with your legs crossed.

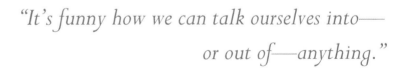

"It's funny how we can talk ourselves into—
or out of—anything."

Lateral Raise

STARTING POSITION

Hold a light dumbbell in each hand. Place your feet shoulder-width apart with your knees slightly bent and pointing straight ahead. Align your body by squaring your hips, drawing your abdominals in, and placing your shoulders down and back. Bring your arms in front of you, allowing them to hang with the elbows slightly bent.

MOVEMENT

Lift the dumbbells directly out to the sides until they reach the level of your shoulders. Pause for a moment and make sure your palms are facing down. Slowly lower your arms and repeat for 12 perfect reps.

The Squeeze Factor

As you raise your arms, squeeze the muscles of your shoulders down.

The Breath Factor

As you exhale, lift your arms out to the sides. As you inhale, lower them slowly.

A Word from Wini

Imagine a pulley on each elbow pulling your arms directly out to the side. As you raise your arms out to the side, draw your shoulders down.

One Size Does Not Fit All

BEGINNER

Practice the movement with no weight at all until
you have mastered the form.

ADVANCED

The way to increase the intensity of this exercise is
to increase the weight until it is challenging to complete 12 reps.

ALTERNATE EXERCISE

If you find you're swinging too much, first practice
the movement sitting on a ball or bench.

Watch Out For

Make sure you are moving from
your shoulders and not your
elbows. If you find you have to
bend your elbows to lift the
weight, try a lighter weight.

Standing Curl

STARTING POSITION

Hold a dumbbell in each hand. Stand with your feet shoulder-width apart and your knees slightly bent and pointing straight ahead. Draw your abdominals in and your shoulders down and back. Place your arms at your sides with the palms facing forward.

MOVEMENT

Keeping your palms facing forward and arms close to your sides, tighten your biceps as you curl both arms up. (The biceps are the muscles in the upper arm that people flex when asked to "make a muscle.") Pause and squeeze the biceps a bit more. Lower slowly. Repeat for 12 perfect reps.

The Squeeze Factor

Start squeezing your biceps muscle as soon as your arm starts curling up. When you get to the top of the curl, contract the muscle even more. Squeeze your biceps up and in with every rep.

The Breath Factor

Exhale as you lift the weight. Inhale as you lower the weight.

A Word from Wini

The arms are working independently, so focus on keeping them even. Unlike an exercise machine, where one side can do more work than the other, standing curls require each arm to "carry its own weight."

One Size Does Not Fit All

BEGINNER

If this exercise irritates your back, try sitting on a chair or exercise ball, as shown.

ADVANCED

The way to increase the intensity of the exercise is to increase the weight until it is challenging to complete 12 reps.

"Don't give up what you want most for what you want at the moment."

Watch Out For

Make sure you don't swing your arms. Keep them very close to your sides, with your midsection tight. If you find yourself rocking back and forth, decrease the amount of weight.

One-Arm Triceps Kickback

STARTING POSITION

Hold a light dumbbell in your right hand. Step your left leg in front of you and bend both knees. Place your left hand on a chair or bench for support. Hinge over from the hips so that your head is in the 2 o'clock position as viewed from the side. Draw your abdominals in and your shoulders down and back. Bend your right arm to a 90-degree angle and lift it slightly above the level of your back. Turn the palm in and press your right arm close to your side, as shown.

MOVEMENT

Keeping the palm facing in and your upper arm glued to your side, extend your elbow until your right arm is in a straight line. Pause and squeeze the muscle on the back of your upper arm (your triceps). Keeping your back still, slowly bend your elbow back to the 90-degree-angle starting position. Repeat for 12 perfect reps. Switch sides.

The Squeeze Factor

Start squeezing your triceps as you extend your arm back. Squeeze the back of your upper arm in and up all the way toward the back of your shoulder.

The Breath Factor

Exhale as you straighten your arm and squeeze your triceps. Inhale as you bend your arm to return to the starting position.

A Word from Wini

Most important to remember is to keep your upper arm absolutely still. Imagine a $100 bill between your arm and your side. Don't let it fly away.

If you are unclear which muscles are your triceps, reach

One Size Does Not Fit All

BEGINNER

Tilt just slightly forward. As your overall strength—including the important core strength—increases, you will be more comfortable leaning over.

ADVANCED

The way to increase the intensity of the exercise is to increase the weight until it is challenging to complete 12 reps.

one arm straight in front of you and bend the elbow to touch your shoulder with your hand. Place your opposite hand on the underside of that arm. Now slowly straighten your elbow and press out, feeling the muscle on the back of the upper arm contract. Say hello to your triceps!

Watch Out For

Make sure you are hinging from your hips and not your waist. No rounding or sagging in the back allowed!

Lengthening Stretch: Back Stretch

STARTING POSITION

Stand tall with your feet hip-width apart. Raise your arms to shoulder height and interlock your fingers.

THE STRETCH

Part one: Reverse your hands so that your palms are facing out. Spread your shoulder blades and reach your arms forward while tucking your tailbone under. Stay here for 5 breaths.

The Breath Factor

As you inhale, reach out from the top of your head to your tailbone. As you exhale, deepen the stretch by reaching your arms forward for part one or up for part two.

A Word from Wini

Focus on the stretch coming from your back and not just your arms. Imagine an energy stream originating at the center of your shoulder blades and going around your back and through your arms with each breath.

Watch Out For

Keep that neck long. The tendency is to hunch the neck. Press your shoulders down and lengthen your spine every time you inhale.

Part two: Raise your arms up, and gently press them up and back. Press your shoulders down, while keeping your arms reaching up. Stay here for 5 breaths.

Upper-Body Basics at a Glance

Each synergy set is designed as a circuit. Do all the exercises or a suggested variation in order with a short rest of 30 to 60 seconds after the entire synergy set is completed. Then repeat for one more complete round before moving on to the next synergy set. By combining the exercises in this way, you'll get a balanced workout that integrates the best strengthening and stretching exercises to keep you lean, long, and strong.

To help track your progress, rewrite or photocopy the Upper-Body Basics Training Log on the opposite page. Then simply fill in the number of reps or breaths of each exercise that you complete. That way, the next time you do this workout, you'll know what you'll have to do to keep progressing. (If you prefer to keep your training logs in a binder, you can find versions of the logs without the photos beginning on page 286.)

SYNERGY SET 1

Close-Grip Row:
12 reps

Prep Pushup:
3 breaths for each part,
3 times

Easy-Open Stretch:
5 breaths

Upper-Body Basics Training Log

Date _____

Synergy Set 1	Reps/Breaths	Round 1	Round 2
Close-Grip Row	12 reps		
Prep Pushup	3 breaths each part, 3 times		
Easy-Open Stretch	5 breaths		
Synergy Set 2			
Lateral Raise	12 reps		
Standing Curl	12 reps		
One-Arm Triceps Kickback	12 reps each arm		
Back Stretch	5 breaths each part		

SYNERGY SET 2

Lateral Raise:
12 reps

Standing Curl:
12 reps

One-Arm Triceps
Kickback: 12 reps
with each arm

Back Stretch:
5 breaths for each part

Upper-Body Intermediate

The next level after Upper-Body Basics, the Upper-Body Intermediate workout takes getting lean, long, and strong up a notch. This routine works on strength, balance, and flexibility in your upper body. You need an exercise ball and a set of weights for this 12-minute routine.

Dumbbell Press on Ball

STARTING POSITION

Sit on the ball with the bottom of the dumbbells on your thighs. Make sure your feet are hip-width apart.

Slowly walk yourself down the ball, bringing the weights up to your shoulders. The ball should be under your shoulders, with your abs tight and your back in a neutral position. Place the dumbbells at the sides of your chest with your elbows out to the sides and slightly below the level of your shoulders. Face your palms forward. Draw your shoulder blades together on the ball while sticking your chest up.

The Squeeze Factor

As you extend your arms up, really squeeze the muscles of your chest up and toward each other while drawing your shoulders down.

The Breath Factor

Exhale as you lift the weight up. Inhale as you lower the weight.

A Word from Wini

To make sure you are working the chest and not just the shoulders, take a moment to really draw your shoulder blades together and press your shoulders down before you begin lifting. Stick that chest up and keep it up the entire movement.

MOVEMENT

Keeping your elbows out to the sides, slowly press your arms up. Bring the dumbbells together, creating a triangle. Lower your elbows slightly below the level of your shoulders to feel a slight stretch in your chest. Repeat for 12 reps.

One Size Does Not Fit All

BEGINNER

Practice getting into the starting position to develop familiarity with working on the ball.

ALTERNATE EXERCISE

The Strong Curves Pushup is a great alternative (see page 224).

Watch Out For

Don't bang the weights together when you bring your arms up. Bring them together very gently.

Lengthening Stretch: Chest Stretch

STARTING POSITION

Sit up on the ball. Arms are at your sides. Abdominals are drawn in and shoulders are down. Your feet are firmly on the floor.

THE STRETCH

Place your arms behind you and lace your fingers together behind your back. Staying upright, reach your arms down and slightly away from you. Hold for 5 slow breaths.

One Size Does Not Fit All

BEGINNER

Place your hands with your palms facing out on the small of your back.

The Breath Factor

As you inhale, make yourself taller by reaching from the top of your head to your tailbone. As you exhale, focus on reaching your arms out and away from you.

A Word from Wini

Think length: long neck, long spine, long arms. As you breathe, feel the breath running through the entire length of your neck, spine, and arms.

Watch Out For

Be careful not to hunch your shoulders up. Relax them down your back.

Pullover on Ball

STARTING POSITION

Sit on the ball with a dumbbell in your hands. Make sure your feet are hip-width apart. Slowly walk yourself down the ball until the ball supports your upper back and neck. Drop your hips so they are below the level of your shoulders. Draw your shoulder blades together and down. Draw your abs in. Press the dumbbell up, as shown, holding it with your arms long and with both palms facing up.

MOVEMENT

Keeping your elbows soft, slowly lower the dumbbell in a wide arc behind your head until you feel a slight stretch in your back. Pause and focus on the muscles in your upper back. Raise the weight slowly up, squeezing your back muscles in and together. Repeat for 12 reps.

One Size Does Not Fit All

BEGINNER

To learn the exercise, try the movement without a dumbbell.

ALTERNATE EXERCISE

Instead of this exercise, you could do the Close-Grip Row (see page 164).

The Squeeze Factor

As you raise the weight up, squeeze the muscles of your back in and together.

The Breath Factor

Inhale as you lower the weight in an arc. Exhale as you lift the weight.

A Word from Wini

Keep those hips down and still as you lower the weight. Imagine that you're strapped into a very small chair.

Watch Out For

Make sure you're moving from your shoulders and not your elbows. Your shoulder blades are initiating the movement and your elbows are merely going along for the ride.

Lengthening Stretch: Pullover Stretch

STARTING POSITION

Sit on the ball with your feet hip-width apart. Slowly walk yourself down the ball until the ball supports your upper back and neck. Drop your hips so they are below the level of your shoulders. Raise your arms toward the ceiling. Feet are firmly on the floor.

THE STRETCH

Lengthen your arms long over your head. Let your arms hang over the ball as you slowly rock back and forth for 5 slow breaths.

One Size Does Not Fit All

BEGINNER

Sit up on the ball and reach your arms up toward the ceiling for 5 breaths.

The Breath Factor

As you inhale, extend your spine by reaching from the top of your head to your tailbone. As you exhale, let your arms and hips drop a little closer to the floor.

A Word from Wini

Take your time and feel your breath moving to all the muscles in your back. Let the weight of your hips and arms naturally increase the stretch.

Watch Out For

Don't overreach your arms. Just breathe and let your body relax into the stretch.

Lying Triceps Extension

STARTING POSITION

Lie faceup with the ball under your shoulders, one light dumbbell in each hand. Feet are shoulder-width apart and firmly on the floor. Shoulders are down and back. Arms are extended up in line with your shoulders. Palms are facing each other.

MOVEMENT

Keeping your upper arms still, slowly lower the dumbbells toward your shoulders. Pause right before the weights touch your shoulders. Slowly extend your forearms back up. Repeat for 12 reps.

One Size Does Not Fit All

BEGINNER

If you're finding it hard to balance, try doing one-arm triceps extensions instead. Use your other arm to support the moving arm.

The Squeeze Factor

As you extend your arms up, squeeze the backs of your upper arms. Visualize the entire lengths of your triceps squeezing together.

The Breath Factor

Inhale as you bend your arms and lower the weight. Exhale as you extend your arms and lift the weight up.

A Word from Wini

Imagine that your upper arms are glued to a shelf. Keep them immobile throughout the entire exercise.

Lengthening Stretch: Seated Triceps Stretch

STARTING POSITION

Sit up on the ball. Abdominals are drawn in and feet are firmly on the floor. Raise your right arm overhead with the palm facing in.

THE STRETCH

Bend your right elbow and touch your shoulder with your hand. Place your left hand on the back of your right upper arm. Gently draw your right arm in close to your ear. Hold for 5 slow breaths. Switch arms.

The Breath Factor

As you inhale, sit up taller by reaching through your spine. As you exhale, gently draw your arm closer to your ear.

A Word from Wini

Try to decrease the space between your forearm and your upper arm. This will increase the stretch in the triceps.

Watch Out For

Be careful not to hunch your shoulders.

One Size Does Not Fit All

BEGINNER

Keep your arm in front of you in line with your shoulder and bend your elbow in to touch your hand to your shoulder.

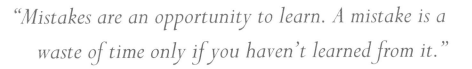

"Mistakes are an opportunity to learn. A mistake is a waste of time only if you haven't learned from it."

Front Raise

STARTING POSITION

Hold a dumbbell in each hand. Place the ball between your lower back and a wall so you can stand against it with your back supported. Place your feet shoulder-width apart, with your knees slightly bent and pointing straight ahead. Align your body by squaring your hips, drawing your abdominals in, and placing your shoulder blades together and down your back. Bring your arms forward, allowing them to extend in front of you, with the elbows slightly bent and palms facing each other.

MOVEMENT

Keeping your elbows slightly bent and your wrists straight, slowly raise the dumbbells up to shoulder height. Pause. Slowly lower your arms and repeat for 12 perfect reps.

The Squeeze Factor

Start squeezing your shoulders back and in as soon as you start lifting your arms.

A Word from Wini

Leaning against the ball corrects the tendency to swing the weights up. It also feels really good on the back.

Watch Out For

Watch out that you don't hunch your shoulders as you raise the weight. You want to be able to keep your shoulders down and your chest up. When in doubt, use a lighter weight to be sure you're doing the movement correctly.

One Size Does Not Fit All

BEGINNER

Practice the movement with one arm at a time, as shown.

ADVANCED

The way to increase the intensity of this exercise is to increase the weight until it is challenging to complete 12 reps.

Lengthening Stretch: Double-Delt Stretch

STARTING POSITION

Hold the ball against the wall at chest height. Feet are shoulder-width apart. Your neck is long, shoulders are down, and abdominals are drawn in.

THE STRETCH

Roll the ball up the wall until you feel a slight stretch in your shoulders. Inhale and lengthen your entire body, keeping your back long. Exhale and gently lean your arms into the ball while keeping your shoulders down. Hold for 5 slow breaths.

The Breath Factor

As you inhale, make yourself taller by reaching through the top of your head. As you exhale, gently press your arms into the ball.

A Word from Wini

Even though you're stretching your shoulders, be sure to keep your shoulder blades down during the entire stretch.

Watch Out For

Don't excessively arch your back. Keeping your abs drawn in and staying close to the wall will help you keep your alignment.

One Size Does Not Fit All

BEGINNER

This stretch can also be done against a wall without the ball.

Leaning Biceps Curl

STARTING POSITION

Hold a dumbbell in each hand. Place the ball be-tween your lower back and a wall so you can stand against it with your back supported. Place your feet shoulder-width apart, with your knees slightly bent and pointing straight ahead. Align your body by squaring your hips, drawing your abdominals in, and placing your shoulder blades together and down your back. Hang your arms at your sides, with the palms facing forward.

MOVEMENT

Press your arms into your sides. Keeping your wrists straight, slowly curl the dumbbells up toward your shoulders. Pause. Slowly lower your arms and re-peat for 12 perfect reps.

The Squeeze Factor

Start squeezing your biceps as you move the weight up. Really pull your biceps up and in.

A Word from Wini

The use of two weights instead of the traditional barbell allows your arms to work indepen-dently. One side cannot do the work of the other.

Watch Out For

Keep your wrists straight. A common tendency is to curl the wrists along with the elbows. The only joint moving should be your elbows.

One Size Does Not Fit All

BEGINNER

Practice the movement with a very light weight until you have mastered the form.

ADVANCED

The way to increase the intensity of this exercise is to increase the weight until it is challenging to complete 12 reps. Make sure your form is perfect before you increase the weight.

"Instead of the words 'I should have,'
substitute 'next time.'"

Lengthening Stretch: Single-Arm Wall Stretch

STARTING POSITION

Step away from the wall so that you can place your hand against the wall with your arm staying in line with your shoulder. Place your palm flat against the wall with your fingers pointing back.

THE STRETCH

Keeping your shoulder down and your arm straight, gently turn away from the wall. Hold for 5 slow breaths. Switch sides.

The Breath Factor

As you inhale, make yourself taller by lengthening from your lower back to your upper chest. As you exhale, gently press your palm into the wall.

A Word from Wini

Think of an energy stream running all the way from your chest through your shoulder and biceps and into the tips of your fingers. Since you're stretching one side at a time, this is a great way to check your flexibility on both sides.

Watch Out For

Be careful not to overstretch by standing too close to the wall or rotating too much.

One Size Does Not Fit All

BEGINNER

This stretch can also be done without the wall by just straightening your arm and reaching it back.

Upper-Body Intermediate at a Glance

Each synergy set is designed as a circuit. Do all the exercises or a suggested variation in order with a short rest of 30 to 60 seconds after the entire synergy set is completed. Then repeat for one more complete round before moving on to the next synergy set. By combining the exercises in this way, you'll get a balanced workout that integrates the best strengthening and stretching exercises to keep you lean, long, and strong.

To help track your progress, rewrite or photocopy the Upper-Body Intermediate Training Log on the opposite page. Then simply fill in the number of reps or breaths of each exercise that you complete. That way, the next time you do this workout, you'll know what you'll have to do to keep progressing. (If you prefer to keep your training logs in a binder, you can find versions of the logs without the photos beginning on page 286.)

SYNERGY SET 1

Dumbbell Press on
Ball: 12 reps

Chest Stretch:
5 breaths

Pullover on Ball:
12 reps

Pullover Stretch:
5 breaths

SYNERGY SET 2

Lying Triceps
Extension: 12 reps

Seated Triceps Stretch:
5 breaths for each arm

Upper-Body Intermediate Training Log

Date _____

Synergy Set 1	Reps/Breaths	Round 1	Round 2
Dumbbell Press on Ball	12 reps		
Chest Stretch	5 breaths		
Pullover on Ball	12 reps		
Pullover Stretch	5 breaths		
Synergy Set 2			
Lying Triceps Extension	12 reps		
Seated Triceps Stretch	5 breaths each arm		
Synergy Set 3			
Front Raise	12 reps		
Double-Delt Stretch	5 breaths		
Leaning Biceps Curl	12 reps		
Single-Arm Wall Stretch	5 breaths each arm		

SYNERGY SET 3

Front Raise:
12 reps

Double-Delt Stretch:
5 breaths

Leaning Biceps Curl:
12 reps

Single-Arm Wall Stretch:
5 breaths for each arm

Upper-Body Challenge

The Upper-Body Challenge workout builds upon the previous routines for the upper body. The exercises flow in a logical sequence, so this routine should take no longer than 12 minutes. All you need for this routine are a set of weights, an exercise ball, and a mat.

Fly and Press

STARTING POSITION

Sit on the ball with the bottom of the dumbbells on your thighs. Make sure your feet are hip-width apart. Slowly walk yourself down the ball, bringing the weights up to your shoulders. The ball should be under your shoulders, with your abs tight and your back in a neutral position. Place the dumbbells at the sides of your chest, with your elbows out slightly below the level of your shoulders. Press your arms up and face your palms toward each other.

MOVEMENT

Part one: Keeping your shoulders down and your elbows slightly bent, slowly bring your arms out in an arc to the sides, as shown. Lower your elbows slightly below the level of your shoulders to feel a slight stretch in your chest. Keeping your chest up, bring your arms together until the weights almost touch. Repeat for 12 reps.

The Squeeze Factor
As you extend your arms up, squeeze your chest together while drawing your shoulders down.

The Breath Factor
Exhale as you lift the weight up. Inhale as you lower the weight.

A Word from Wini
In part one of this exercise, you keep your elbows still and move only from the shoulders with your palms facing each other to create an arc shape. In part two, you bend your elbows to have the

Part two: Immediately bring your arms back up and face your palms front.

Then bend your elbows out to the sides to create a square with your arms. Repeat for 12 reps.

One Size Does Not Fit All

BEGINNER

Just try the dumbbell presses by themselves.

ADVANCED

The way to increase the intensity of this exercise is to increase the weight until it is challenging to complete 12 reps.

ALTERNATE EXERCISE

Instead of this exercise, you could do the Strong Curves Pushup (see page 224), as shown.

Watch Out For

muscles in your arms assist you more and create a square shape.

Make sure the weights aren't too heavy. If you find that you need to bend your elbows in part one, use a lighter weight. Keep the top of your head reaching long to avoid tension in your neck. To avoid hunch-

ing your shoulders, pull your shoulder blades down and toward each other.

Lengthening Stretch: Up-and-Over Stretch

STARTING POSITION

Sit up on the ball and lace your hands behind your back. Abdominals are drawn in and shoulders are down. Feet are firmly on the floor.

THE STRETCH

Reach your arms down and slightly away from you. Keeping your shoulders down, raise your arms up behind you and lean over the ball, resting your chest on your thighs. Hold for 5 slow breaths.

One Size Does Not Fit All

BEGINNER

Do the first part only. Lace your fingers together behind your back and reach your arms down and away from you.

The Breath Factor

As you inhale, lengthen your spine and reach your arms up and away from you. As you exhale, drop your head and relax your back.

A Word from Wini

This is a great stretch for the chest, shoulders, biceps, and lower back. If your mind is wandering during your workout, use this stretch to bring your focus back to your breath and body.

Watch Out For

Make sure your chest is supported on your thighs. Be sure to drop your head and relax your neck.

Row on Ball

STARTING POSITION

Lie facedown on an exercise ball with the ball beneath your torso. Place your feet hip-width apart on the floor and press your heels back. Draw in your abs and lengthen your back. Hold a dumbbell in each hand. Bring your arms in line with your shoulders. Your palms are facing back.

MOVEMENT

Draw your shoulder blades together and your elbows up until they move past the level of your back to create a square shape. As your elbows pass the level of your back, pause for a moment. Slowly lower your arms and repeat for 12 perfect reps.

One Size Does Not Fit All

BEGINNER

Try the movement without the weight. Practice lying on the ball and lifting your arms up.

ADVANCED

Increase the weight until it is challenging to complete 12 reps.

The Squeeze Factor

Start squeezing your upper-back muscles in and together as soon as you initiate the movement. Remember to squeeze as you are moving, and then when your elbows go beyond the level of your shoulders, give an extra contraction.

The Breath Factor

Exhale as you lift your arms up to create a square shape. Inhale as you lower your arms.

A Word from Wini

Try to keep your abs drawn in during the entire movement. Keeping your abs in is never about holding your breath; it's about holding your posture.

Watch Out For

Make sure your elbows are traveling out to the sides and not toward your hips. Keep your neck long and eyes toward the floor.

Lengthening Stretch: Side Stretch

STARTING POSITION

Sit on the ball and then slowly walk yourself down it until the ball supports your upper back and neck. Drop your hips so they are below the level of your shoulders. Your feet are firmly on the floor and hip-width apart. Lengthen your arms long over your head.

THE STRETCH

Grab your right wrist with your left hand and gently pull toward the left. Hold for 5 breaths. Switch sides.

The Breath Factor

As you inhale, make yourself taller by reaching from your upper chest through your lower back. As you exhale, gently reach through the side being stretched.

A Word from Wini

When you extend one side, think about a string pulling you from your hip all the way through the tips of your fingers.

Watch Out For

Don't overreach your arms. Keep your shoulders down even though you are extending your arms.

One Size Does Not Fit All

BEGINNER

Sit up on the ball and reach your arms up and together toward the ceiling. Take your right wrist in your left hand and stretch gently up and toward the left. Hold for 5 breaths. Switch sides.

"Understand that you are capable of making significant changes. Then prove yourself right."

Y Rear Lateral

STARTING POSITION

Lie facedown on an exercise ball with the ball beneath your torso. Bring your feet to hip-width apart. Draw in your abs and lengthen your back. Hold a very light dumbbell in each hand. Walk your arms slightly forward until they are at 11 o'clock and 1 o'clock.

MOVEMENT

Draw your shoulder blades together and your arms up until they are level with your shoulders. As you create a Y shape, pause for a moment. Slowly lower your arms and repeat for 12 perfect reps.

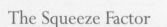

The Squeeze Factor

Start squeezing the muscles in the back of your shoulders as soon as you initiate the movement. When your arms reach the level of your shoulders, squeeze your shoulders in toward the midline of your body.

The Breath Factor

Exhale as you lift your arms to create a Y shape. Inhale as you lower your arms.

A Word from Wini

Go light with the weights. This is a very difficult exercise, and the weight is at the end of a long lever (your arm). The farther away the weight is from you, the more difficult it is going to be.

One Size Does Not Fit All

BEGINNER

If this exercise is too difficult, try taking your arms directly out to your sides, as shown, instead of slightly forward.

ADVANCED

The way to increase the intensity of this exercise is to increase the weight until it is challenging to complete 12 reps.

Watch Out For

Keep your neck long to avoid straining it. Imagine a long line running from your tailbone through the top of your head. Try to stay relaxed and avoid hyperextending your neck or letting it hang down. Keep your body in a long, fluid line.

Lengthening Stretch: Eagle Arms

STARTING POSITION

Sit up on the ball. Align your body by squaring your hips, drawing your abdominals in, and placing your shoulders down and back. Your feet are firmly on the floor. Extend your arms straight out to the sides in line with your shoulders.

THE STRETCH

Bending both elbows in toward your chest, hook your left arm under your right arm above the elbow. Place your left hand across your right wrist. Raise both elbows up. Hold for 5 breaths. Extend your arms back out to the sides. Switch sides.

The Breath Factor

As you inhale, lengthen the area between your upper chest and lower back. As you exhale, gently lift your elbows up.

A Word from Wini

When you extend your arms at the start and in between sides, really reach all the way out through your hands.

Watch Out For

Try not to cave in by rounding your shoulders forward. Keep your shoulders down. Place them down your back before you hook your arms and then take a moment to place them down again before you raise your elbows.

One Size Does Not Fit All

BEGINNER

Hook your left arm under your right triceps and take your right arm gently across your chest. Hold for 5 breaths. Switch sides.

"Training strengthens the mind. The physical is merely a side effect."

Kickback on Ball

STARTING POSITION

Lie facedown on an exercise ball with the ball beneath your torso. Your feet should be hip-width apart. Draw in your abs and lengthen your back. Hold a very light dumbbell in each hand. Draw your shoulders down and back. Turn your palms in with your arms hanging down at your sides. Lift your upper arms toward the sides of your body while keeping your elbows bent to form a 90-degree angle.

MOVEMENT

Keeping your palms facing each other and your arms glued to your sides, extend your elbows until your arms are in a straight line. Pause and squeeze your triceps. Slowly bend your elbows back to the 90-degree starting position. Repeat for 12 perfect reps.

The Squeeze Factor

Start squeezing your triceps as you straighten your arms. Imagine squeezing each triceps in toward the center of your arm and up toward your shoulder.

The Breath Factor

Exhale as you extend your arms and lift the weights up. Inhale as you bend your arms back to a 90-degree angle.

A Word from Wini

Imagine a stick lying across your back that your elbows are hooked on. Keep those elbows up as you extend and lower your arms.

One Size Does Not Fit All

BEGINNER

Try the movement without the weight, as shown. Practice lying on the ball and extending your arms. Remember to squeeze your triceps.

ADVANCED

The way to increase the intensity of this exercise is to increase the weight until it is challenging to complete 12 reps.

Watch Out For

Don't slump on the ball. Think about keeping your belly button off the ball and your back long.

Lengthening Stretch: Cobra on Ball

STARTING POSITION

Lie facedown on an exercise ball with the ball beneath your torso. Lengthen your legs and place them slightly more than hip-width apart. Press the balls of your feet into the floor for support. Lace your fingers together behind your back.

THE STRETCH

Draw your navel in and raise your torso in a straight line from your hips through the top of your head. Keeping your hands interlocked, straighten your arms. Hold for 5 slow breaths.

The Breath Factor

As you inhale, lengthen from the balls of your feet through the top of your head. As you exhale, roll your shoulders back and reach your arms behind you.

A Word from Wini

Don't worry about lifting your arms up. The key here is to really reach out. With every breath, increase the space between your head and your feet. Besides getting a great stretch for the upper body, you are strengthening the entire length of your back by holding your body in a straight line.

One Size Does Not Fit All

BEGINNER

Try the same movement on a mat instead of the ball.

"Victory is not about never failing. Victory is starting again if you have a slip. It is getting up one more time."

Watch Out For

Make sure your legs are slightly wider than your hips to keep you stable.

Angled Biceps Curl on Ball

STARTING POSITION

Sit on the ball with a dumbbell in each hand. Abs are drawn in, hips are even, and shoulders are relaxed. Your feet are hip-width apart and firmly on the floor. Arms are at your sides with your palms facing forward.

MOVEMENT

Press your upper arms into your sides. Leading with the pinky end of your hand, curl the weight up. Pause on top. Keep your arms close to your sides as you lower the weight slowly. Repeat for 12 perfect reps.

The Squeeze Factor

As you curl your arms up, squeeze the insides of your biceps. Squeeze the biceps in and up the arm.

The Breath Factor

Exhale as you bend your arms and lift the weight up. Inhale as you lengthen your arms and lower the weight down.

A Word from Wini

See if you can really feel the inside part of your biceps by truly leading with the pinky end of the dumbbell. Try it without the weight and with one hand on your arm. Yes, that is your biceps!

One Size Does Not Fit All

BEGINNER

Try the movement standing up, as shown. Really press your arms into your sides as you curl the weight up.

ADVANCED

The way to increase the intensity of this exercise is to increase the weight until it is challenging to complete 12 reps.

Watch Out For

Make sure you go through the entire range of motion, yet be careful not to hyperextend your elbows. The elbows should have a slight bend in them at the end of the movement.

Lengthening Stretch: Child's Pose on Ball

STARTING POSITION

Kneel on a mat with the ball in front of you.
Place your hands on the ball.

THE STRETCH

Slowly sit back on your heels and drop
your head. Roll the ball away from you
by extending your arms. Hold for
5 slow breaths.

The Breath Factor

As you inhale, lengthen your
spine by increasing the space
between your head and your
tailbone. As you exhale, drop
your hips and head down and
relax into the stretch.

A Word from Wini

This is a great way to end the
workout. Focus on breathing
into the areas of your body that
are holding any stress.

Watch Out For

Make sure your arms are relaxed on the ball and not
pressing with force.

One Size Does Not Fit All

ALTERNATE EXERCISE

Instead of the Child's Pose on Ball, try doing a regular Child's Pose (see page 38).

*"The days you can't find 12 minutes to exercise
are the days you need 30 minutes."*

Upper-Body Challenge at a Glance

Each synergy set is designed as a circuit. Do all the exercises or a suggested variation in order with a short rest of 30 to 60 seconds after the entire synergy set is completed. Then repeat for one more complete round before moving on to the next synergy set. By combining the exercises in this way, you'll get a balanced workout that integrates the best strengthening and stretching exercises to keep you lean, long, and strong.

To help track your progress, rewrite or photocopy the Upper-Body Challenge Training Log on the opposite page. Then simply fill in the number of reps or breaths of each exercise that you complete. That way, the next time you do this workout, you'll know what you'll have to do to keep progressing. (If you prefer to keep your training logs in a binder, you can find versions of the logs without the photos beginning on page 286.)

SYNERGY SET 1

Fly and Press: 12 reps for each movement

Up-and-Over Stretch: 5 breaths

Row on Ball: 12 reps

Side Stretch: 5 breaths on each side

Upper-Body Challenge Training Log

Date _____

Synergy Set 1		Round 1	Round 2
Fly and Press	12 reps each movement		
Up-and-Over Stretch	5 breaths		
Row on Ball	12 reps		
Side Stretch	5 breaths each side		
Synergy Set 2			
Y Rear Lateral	12 reps		
Eagle Arms	5 breaths each side		
Kickback on Ball	12 reps		
Cobra on Ball	5 breaths		
Angled Biceps Curl on Ball	12 reps		
Child's Pose on Ball	5 breaths		

SYNERGY SET 2

| Y Rear Lateral: 12 reps | Eagle Arms: 5 breaths on each side | Kickback on Ball: 12 reps | Cobra on Ball: 5 breaths | Angled Biceps Curl on Ball: 12 reps | Child's Pose on Ball: 5 breaths |

Upper-Body Express

Upper-Body Express is a 6-minute routine that really flows. You need just a set of dumbbells, a mat, and a towel. No need for an exercise ball for this workout. You can do this when you are pressed for time, traveling, or just want an efficient, balanced upper-body routine.

Strong Curves Pushup

STARTING POSITION

Start by kneeling on a mat. Place a rolled-up towel in between your thighs. Place your hands down a little wider than your shoulders, with your fingers pointing straight ahead and your palms flat down. Walk your legs out until they are straight, with your toes on the mat. Your body is now in a straight line from your head and shoulders through your hips all the way to your ankles. Look at a spot slightly ahead of you on the floor.

MOVEMENT

Gently squeeze the towel between your legs. Lower yourself slowly, with your elbows traveling out to the sides. Stop 1 inch away from the mat. Push the floor away from you as you straighten your arms to come up. Complete 8 reps and add 1 rep with each workout until you can do 12.

The Squeeze Factor

Contract your chest muscles as you come up. Keeping your shoulders down, squeeze your chest muscles in and toward each other.

The Breath Factor

Inhale as you lower yourself toward the mat. Exhale as you push up and press the floor down.

A Word from Wini

Squeeze the towel to help you feel how the abs truly are integrated into the exercise. Imagine your inner thighs drawing the towel up and in toward your center.

One Size Does Not Fit All

BEGINNER

Try these with your knees on the mat. Work on keeping your body in a straight line from your shoulders through your knees.

ADVANCED

The way to increase the intensity of pushups is to add a gravity challenge. Try elevating your feet on a small stool or box. Remember, abs in!

Watch Out For

The priority is that your body is in a straight line from your shoulders through your hips all the way to your heels. There should be no bending at the waist or hips. Work on your alignment first; the strength will come as the workouts pile up.

Bent-Over Row

STARTING POSITION

Hold a dumbbell in each hand. Align your feet shoulder-width apart, with your knees pointing straight ahead. Hinging at your hips, bend over, keeping your back long by tightening your abs and very slightly arching your lower back. Your torso should be a few inches above parallel to the floor. Keep your knees slightly bent and your back slightly arched to protect it. Draw your abdominals in and your shoulders down and back. Turn your palms to face the wall behind you.

MOVEMENT

Keeping your palms back, create a square shape by lifting your elbows out to the sides. Draw your elbows up and to the sides until they move past the level of your back. As your arms pass the level of your back, pause for a moment. Slowly lower your arms and repeat for 12 perfect reps.

The Squeeze Factor

Start squeezing your upper back as well as your biceps as soon as you start moving your elbows. When your elbows come above your back, squeeze the muscles of your back toward each other.

The Breath Factor

Exhale as you lift the weight up. Inhale as you lower the weight.

A Word from Wini

You want to feel this in your upper back, not just your arms. Draw your shoulder blades together to really connect to the muscles of your back.

One Size Does Not Fit All

BEGINNER

If this exercise bothers your lower back, raise your body up a few inches, as shown. As you build your core strength, it will get easier.

ADVANCED

The way to increase the intensity of this exercise is to increase the weight until it is challenging to complete 12 reps.

Watch Out For

Be careful not to round your back. You want your back to be long and slightly arched. Remember: The bend is created at the hips, not the waist.

Lengthening Stretch: Laced-Hands Stretch

STARTING POSITION

Stand tall with your feet hip-width apart and your knees slightly bent. Lace your fingers together behind your back.

THE STRETCH

Lengthen your arms long toward the floor behind you. Tilting at your hips, drop your head down and raise your arms up and away from you. Stay here for 5 breaths.

One Size Does Not Fit All

BEGINNER

Just do the first part of the stretch by lacing your fingers together behind your back and lengthening your arms.

The Breath Factor

As you inhale, think about extending from the top of your head to the tip of your tailbone. As you exhale, reach your arms up and together.

A Word from Wini

Feel your chest opening as you reach your arms back. Feel your lower back releasing as you tilt over.

Watch Out For

Don't overreach your arms. Just breathe and let your body relax into the stretch.

Double-Triceps Kickback

STARTING POSITION

Hold a light dumbbell in each hand. Stand with your feet shoulder-width apart. Draw your abdominals in and relax your shoulders down and back. Turn your palms in with your arms hanging down at your sides. Hinging at your hips, bend over, keeping your back long by drawing in your abs and very slightly arching your lower back. Your torso should be above parallel to the floor. Lift your upper arms to press against the sides of your body while keeping your elbows bent to form a 90-degree angle.

MOVEMENT

Keeping your palms facing each other and arms glued to your sides, extend your elbows until your arms are in a straight line. Pause and squeeze your triceps. Keeping your torso still, slowly bend your elbows back to the 90-degree starting position. Repeat for 12 perfect reps.

One Size Does Not Fit All

BEGINNER

For an easier version, do One-Arm Triceps Kickbacks (see page 174).

ADVANCED

Increase the weight until it is challenging to complete 12 reps.

The Squeeze Factor

Start squeezing your triceps as you extend your arms back. Imagine you are wringing out the last bit of water from a sponge at the back of your upper arms.

The Breath Factor

Exhale as you extend your arms up to lift the weight. Inhale as you bend your arms to lower the weight.

Watch Out For

Keep your back long and your abs tight at all times. If you feel this in your lower back, make sure your knees are slightly bent and raise your torso up a few inches.

Standing Constant Curl

STARTING POSITION

Hold a dumbbell in each hand. Align your feet shoulder-width apart, with your knees slightly bent and pointing straight ahead. Draw your abdominals in and your shoulders down and back. Turn your palms to face forward, with your arms hanging down in front of you.

MOVEMENT

Keeping your palms facing forward and your arms close to your sides, curl your left arm up, as shown, keeping your right arm down. As you lower your left arm, simultaneously start curling your right arm. Continue this way with your arms constantly moving and passing each other at about waist level. Repeat for 12 perfect reps on each arm.

The Squeeze Factor

Start squeezing your biceps muscle as soon as the arm starts curling up. When you get to the top of the curl, contract a little extra.

The Breath Factor

This exercise requires constant lifting, so breathe naturally with each movement. If you find you are holding your breath, just start counting aloud.

A Word from Wini

Constant movement curls develop strength, balance, and co-ordination. Not only are your biceps working, your abs are working to keep you in perfect alignment.

One Size Does Not Fit All

BEGINNER

If this exercise bothers your back, try sitting on a chair, bench, or exercise ball, as shown.

ADVANCED

The way to increase the intensity of this exercise is to increase the weight until it is challenging to complete 12 reps.

Watch Out For

There should be no swinging at all. Keep your arms very close to your sides and your abs tight. If you find yourself rocking back and forth or side to side, lower the weight.

Lengthening Stretch: Two-Part Arm Stretch

STARTING POSITION

Place your feet shoulder-width apart with your knees slightly bent and pointing straight ahead. Align your body by squaring your hips, drawing your abdominals in, and placing your shoulders down and back. Place your left arm straight out to the side, in line with your shoulder.

THE STRETCH

First reach out and press your left hand back to feel a stretch in your biceps. Hold for 3 breaths. Then take your left arm across your body, drawing it in toward your chest with your right arm, as shown. Hold for 3 breaths. Switch arms.

The Breath Factor

As you inhale, think about extending from the top of your head to the tip of your tailbone. As you exhale, relax your shoulders and arms deeper into each stretch.

A Word from Wini

For the first part, really extend out with the heel of your hand for a great stretch along the entire front of the arm. For the second part, really breathe into the entire back of the arm all the way into your shoulder.

Watch Out For

Keep your shoulders held down when you take your arm across your body. Place them down your back before you hook your arm.

One Size Does Not Fit All

BEGINNER

Take your arm across your body without hooking
your other arm underneath.

*"Strength does not come from how much weight
you can lift or how many miles you can run.
Strength comes from knowing that you set a goal and
rose to the challenge. Strength comes from within."*

Upper-Body Express at a Glance

Each synergy set is designed as a circuit. Do all the exercises or a suggested variation in order with a short rest of 30 to 60 seconds after the entire synergy set is completed. Then repeat for one more complete round before moving on to the next synergy set. By combining the exercises in this way, you'll get a balanced workout that integrates the best strengthening and stretching exercises to keep you lean, long, and strong.

To help track your progress, rewrite or photocopy the Upper-Body Express Training Log on the opposite page. Then simply fill in the number of reps or breaths of each exercise that you complete. That way, the next time you do this workout, you'll know what you'll have to do to keep progressing. (If you prefer to keep your training logs in a binder, you can find versions of the logs without the photos beginning on page 286.)

SYNERGY SET 1

Strong Curves
Pushup: 8–12 reps

Bent-Over Row:
12 reps

Laced-Hands Stretch:
5 breaths

Upper-Body Express Training Log

Date _____

Synergy Set 1	Reps/Breaths	Round 1	Round 2
Strong Curves Pushup	8–12 reps		
Bent-Over Row	12 reps		
Laced-Hands Stretch	5 breaths		

Synergy Set 2			
Double-Triceps Kickback	12 reps		
Standing Constant Curl	12 reps each arm		
Two-Part Arm Stretch	3 breaths each movement		

SYNERGY SET 2

Double-Triceps
Kickback: 12 reps

Standing Constant
Curl: 12 reps with
each arm

Two-Part Arm
Stretch: 3 breaths for
each movement

PART THREE

YOUR CUSTOM MAP: DESIGNING YOUR PROGRAM

CHOOSING YOUR FOCUS

The precision workouts in this book are designed to get you visible results in just 6 weeks. The question is: What kind of results do you want?

We're all unique, and your fitness goals may be very different from the goals of your best friend, colleague, or sister. Maybe you want to tighten your glutes or banish your belly. Maybe your goal is to have toned arms that look great in sleeveless shirts and dresses. Or maybe you just want to build up some strength and lose some weight.

One size does not fit all, and that's especially true when it comes to exercise programs. That's why I've developed customized workout programs specially designed to help you meet your individual fitness goals. All you need to do is choose your focus, follow the appropriate plan, and enjoy the targeted results you'll soon achieve. Here are the four focus plans.

◆ Fat-Blasting Focus
◆ Core Focus
◆ Lower-Body Focus
◆ Upper-Body Focus

If you haven't been exercising regularly, I recommend that you start with the Fat-Blasting Focus Program. This program will work out your entire body equally, and it's a great way to jump-start weight loss.

If you're already a regular exerciser or are eager to start getting targeted results, you can jump ahead to one of the other focus plans. If you're unsure which plan to pick, turn to pages 241, 244, 247, and 250 for a set of guidelines that will help you decide.

Each focus program includes 6-week basic, intermediate, challenge, and express workout routines. Unless you've been working out consistently up to this point, start with the basic level. From there, you can progress at your own pace. On days when you're rushed for time, try the express workout, which can be done in just 5 to 8 minutes with minimal equipment.

Finally, even if you choose the Core, Lower-Body, or Upper-Body Focus Program, you don't need to worry that you'll be neglecting the rest of your body. These programs are designed to benefit your entire body—they just provide a little extra focus where you need it most. For example, in the Core Focus Program, you'll still be doing one lower-body workout and one upper-body workout each week, but you'll double up on your core workouts, giving you that flatter stomach you've been wishing for.

Why is it important to train the entire body? There are four key reasons.

Aesthetic balance. It's simple: A strong and toned upper body to match a strong and toned lower body looks better. Women tend to want to focus on their lower bodies more. Yet when you work your upper body, your sculpted shoulders and better posture will make your lower body look even better.

Strength balance. I understand the desire for a flat stomach. Yet strength is essential for your entire body, not just your abs. Being able to carry the groceries, climb the stairs, and sit at your desk without back pain is even more important than looking good in your clothes.

Injury prevention. Training your whole body helps to protect you against injury. For example, even if your goal is to firm up your thighs, you'll still want to do some lower-back and abdominal exercises, which will strengthen you against weak abdominals and lower-back pain. Likewise, doing some exercises that target your upper body will improve your posture—a bonus no matter what your target area. And finally, the exercises found in the lower-body routines will improve your leg strength and flexibility, helping you bend and pick up your kids without having to worry about pulling a muscle or getting tired.

Life balance. Just as the synergy set workouts help to balance you physically by adding stretches to complement the strength moves, having a balanced approach to your overall training tends to spill over into other areas of your life. The way you do anything is the way you do everything.

KEEPING THE FOCUS

As I already mentioned, each level of the focus programs takes 6 weeks to complete. You might be tempted to skip around, changing the workout each day or shortening the number of weeks you do any one program. But I strongly encourage you to stick to just one plan for the full 6 weeks.

By doing so, you're giving your body the time it needs to get strong, focused results. If you keep your program the same, working out your body consistently, then what changes is *you*. Gradually, you'll find yourself using better form to complete the exercises, using a heavier weight, or holding each stretch for an additional breath. Sticking with the same program for 6 weeks gives you a mirror in which you can watch yourself improve. If you take a piece of metal and rub it in the same place consistently, it eventually will bend. Likewise, when you stick with one focus program for a minimum of 6 weeks, the concentrated effort you devote to your goal is sure to pay off with targeted results.

The Fat-Blasting Focus Program

This program is for you if:

- You want to focus on sculpting your entire body.
- You are just starting to exercise and want to build a base of strength.
- You want to focus on overall weight loss without picking a focus area.
- You completed a focus program on your upper body, lower body, or core and now want to maintain those results.

Keep the following points in mind as you begin the Fat-Blasting Focus Program.

- I have assigned the workouts to Monday, Tuesday, Thursday, and Friday of each week, but you can move your workouts to other days in the week if those are more convenient for you, or if you have more time to exercise on the weekend.
- The Fat-Blasting Focus Program is four workouts a week, with one workout for each of the three focus areas and the fourth workout alternating each week.
- Include a precision warmup for every workout by doing one easy circuit of the entire program to warm up your body for the specific routine ahead of you.
- Include a Precision Cardio workout two or three times each week. You can do your cardio workouts on the days you do your synergy set workouts or on your off days.
- Stay accountable by filling in your training logs. Be sure to record the number of reps or breaths you completed for each exercise or stretch. That way, you'll know what you need to do next time to continue to improve.
- When short on time, or while traveling, you can substitute an express workout.
- Each workout requires an investment of approximately 12 minutes. The days you can't find 12 minutes to do something positive for yourself are the days you deserve it most.

FAT-BLASTING FOCUS: BASIC PROGRAM

- Stay with the program a minimum of 6 weeks. After 6 weeks, you can repeat it or move on to the intermediate level.
- Remember that if an exercise is too challenging for you right now, you can do the beginner modification instead.

- Don't forget to stay hydrated as you work out. Be sure you have a water bottle nearby, and sip from it frequently.
- Include two or three Precision Cardio workouts per week.

Week	Monday	Tuesday	Wednesday	Thursday	Friday
1	Core Basics	Lower-Body Basics	—	Upper-Body Basics	Core Basics
2	Lower-Body Basics	Upper-Body Basics	—	Core Basics	Lower-Body Basics
3	Upper-Body Basics	Core Basics	—	Lower-Body Basics	Upper-Body Basics
4	Core Basics	Lower-Body Basics	—	Upper-Body Basics	Core Basics
5	Lower-Body Basics	Upper-Body Basics	—	Core Basics	Lower-Body Basics
6	Upper-Body Basics	Core Basics	—	Lower-Body Basics	Upper-Body Basics

FAT-BLASTING FOCUS: INTERMEDIATE PROGRAM

- This program is the next level of the Fat-Blasting Focus Program.
- Stay with this plan for a minimum of 6 weeks. That will take you through eight workouts each for the upper body, lower body, and core.

- After 6 weeks, you can repeat the program or move on to the next level.
- Include two or three Precision Cardio workouts per week.

Week	Monday	Tuesday	Wednesday	Thursday	Friday
1	Core Intermediate	Lower-Body Intermediate	—	Upper-Body Intermediate	Core Intermediate
2	Lower-Body Intermediate	Upper-Body Intermediate	—	Core Intermediate	Lower-Body Intermediate
3	Upper-Body Intermediate	Core Intermediate	—	Lower-Body Intermediate	Upper-Body Intermediate
4	Core Intermediate	Lower-Body Intermediate	—	Upper-Body Intermediate	Core Intermediate
5	Lower-Body Intermediate	Upper-Body Intermediate	—	Core Intermediate	Lower-Body Intermediate
6	Upper-Body Intermediate	Core Intermediate	—	Lower-Body Intermediate	Upper-Body Intermediate

Fat-Blasting Focus: Challenge Program

- This program is the advanced level of the Fat-Blasting Focus Program.
- Stay with this plan for a minimum of 6 weeks. Remember that every workout is an opportunity to improve.
- Include two or three Precision Cardio workouts per week.

- Some of the exercises in these workouts may be particularly challenging. If they're too tough at first, try the beginner option that's offered for each exercise. As you progress, you can move from the easier options to the more challenging ones.

Week	Monday	Tuesday	Wednesday	Thursday	Friday
1	Core Challenge	Lower-Body Challenge	—	Upper-Body Challenge	Core Challenge
2	Lower-Body Challenge	Upper-Body Challenge	—	Core Challenge	Lower-Body Challenge
3	Upper-Body Challenge	Core Challenge	—	Lower-Body Challenge	Upper-Body Challenge
4	Core Challenge	Lower-Body Challenge	—	Upper-Body Challenge	Core Challenge
5	Lower-Body Challenge	Upper-Body Challenge	—	Core Challenge	Lower-Body Challenge
6	Upper-Body Challenge	Core Challenge	—	Lower-Body Challenge	Upper-Body Challenge

Fat-Blasting Focus: Express Program

- This program is for you if you want a quick and effective plan with a minimum of equipment.
- The express workouts can be done whenever you are pressed for time. Or you can use them in a 6-week program, as shown here.
- Include two or three Precision Cardio workouts per week.

Week	Monday	Tuesday	Wednesday	Thursday	Friday
1	Core Express	Lower-Body Express	—	Upper-Body Express	Core Express
2	Lower-Body Express	Upper-Body Express	—	Core Express	Lower-Body Express
3	Upper-Body Express	Core Express	—	Lower-Body Express	Upper-Body Express
4	Core Express	Lower-Body Express	—	Upper-Body Express	Core Express
5	Lower-Body Express	Upper-Body Express	—	Core Express	Lower-Body Express
6	Upper-Body Express	Core Express	—	Lower-Body Express	Upper-Body Express

The Core Focus Program

The Core Focus Program targets your abdominal and lower-back muscles, which are used in everything you do, from lifting to walking. All movement starts with your center.

This focus program is for you if:

- You consider your midsection your challenge area.
- You want to improve your core strength for everyday activities.
- You want to strengthen your abdominals and reduce lower-back pain.
- You've been having a hard time strengthening your stomach muscles after having a baby.
- You want to work on your whole body yet believe your midsection could use a little extra help.

Keep the following points in mind as you begin the Core Focus Program.

- I have assigned the workouts to Monday, Tuesday, Thursday, and Friday of each week, but you can move your workouts to other days in the week if those are more convenient for you, or if you have more time to exercise on the weekend.

- The Core Focus Program consists of four workouts a week, with one workout each for the upper body and lower body and two workouts for the core. You get the benefits of a full-body workout with an extra core workout to emphasize those abs.
- Include a precision warmup for every workout by doing one easy circuit of the entire program to warm up your body for the specific routine ahead of you.
- Include a Precision Cardio workout two or three times a week. You can do your cardio workouts on the days you do your synergy set workouts or on your off days.
- Stay accountable by filling in your training logs. Be sure to record the number of reps or breaths you completed for each exercise or stretch. That way, you'll know what you need to do next time to continue to improve.
- Remember that each workout requires an investment of 12 minutes or less. The days you can't find 12 minutes to work out are the days you should give yourself a half-hour!
- When you're short on time or traveling, you can substitute an express workout.

Core Focus: Basic Program

- Stay with the program a minimum of 6 weeks. After 6 weeks, you can repeat it or move on to the intermediate level.
- Remember that if an exercise is too challenging for you right now, you can do the beginner modification instead.
- Don't forget to stay hydrated as you work out. Be sure you have a water bottle nearby, and sip from it frequently.
- Include two or three Precision Cardio workouts per week.

Week	Monday	Tuesday	Wednesday	Thursday	Friday
1	Core Basics	Lower-Body Basics	—	Upper-Body Basics	Core Basics
2	Lower-Body Basics	Core Basics	—	Upper-Body Basics	Core Basics
3	Upper-Body Basics	Core Basics	—	Lower-Body Basics	Core Basics
4	Core Basics	Lower-Body Basics	—	Upper-Body Basics	Core Basics
5	Lower-Body Basics	Core Basics	—	Upper-Body Basics	Core Basics
6	Upper-Body Basics	Core Basics	—	Lower-Body Basics	Core Basics

Core Focus: Intermediate Program

- This program is the next level of the Core Focus Program.
- Stay with this plan for a minimum of 6 weeks. That will take you through 12 core workouts and 6 lower-body and upper-body workouts.
- After 6 weeks, you can repeat the program or move on to the next level.
- Include two or three Precision Cardio workouts per week.

Week	Monday	Tuesday	Wednesday	Thursday	Friday
1	Core Intermediate	Lower-Body Intermediate	—	Upper-Body Intermediate	Core Intermediate
2	Lower-Body Intermediate	Core Intermediate	—	Upper-Body Intermediate	Core Intermediate
3	Upper-Body Intermediate	Core Intermediate	—	Lower-Body Intermediate	Core Intermediate
4	Core Intermediate	Lower-Body Intermediate	—	Upper-Body Intermediate	Core Intermediate
5	Lower-Body Intermediate	Core Intermediate	—	Upper-Body Intermediate	Core Intermediate
6	Upper-Body Intermediate	Core Intermediate	—	Lower-Body Intermediate	Core Intermediate

CORE FOCUS: CHALLENGE PROGRAM

- This program is the advanced level of the Core Focus Program.
- Stay with this plan for a minimum of 6 weeks. That will be 12 core workouts and 6 lower-body and upper-body workouts.
- Include two or three Precision Cardio workouts per week.

- Some of the exercises in these workouts may be particularly challenging. If they're too tough at first, try the beginner option that's offered for each exercise. As you progress, you can move from the easier options to the more challenging ones.

Week	Monday	Tuesday	Wednesday	Thursday	Friday
1	Core Challenge	Lower-Body Challenge	—	Upper-Body Challenge	Core Challenge
2	Lower-Body Challenge	Core Challenge	—	Upper-Body Challenge	Core Challenge
3	Upper-Body Challenge	Core Challenge	—	Lower-Body Challenge	Core Challenge
4	Core Challenge	Lower-Body Challenge	—	Upper-Body Challenge	Core Challenge
5	Lower-Body Challenge	Core Challenge	—	Upper-Body Challenge	Core Challenge
6	Upper-Body Challenge	Core Challenge	—	Lower-Body Challenge	Core Challenge

CORE FOCUS: EXPRESS PROGRAM

- This program is for you if you want a quick and effective plan with a minimum of equipment.
- The express workouts can be done whenever you're pressed for time. Or you can use them in a 6-week program, as shown here.
- Include two or three Precision Cardio workouts per week.

Week	Monday	Tuesday	Wednesday	Thursday	Friday
1	Core Express	Lower-Body Express	—	Upper-Body Express	Core Express
2	Lower-Body Express	Core Express	—	Upper-Body Express	Core Express
3	Upper-Body Express	Core Express	—	Lower-Body Express	Core Express
4	Core Express	Lower-Body Express	—	Upper-Body Express	Core Express
5	Lower-Body Express	Core Express	—	Upper-Body Express	Core Express
6	Upper-Body Express	Core Express	—	Lower-Body Express	Core Express

The Lower-Body Focus Program

The Lower-Body Focus Program is for you if:

- You have always considered your lower body your problem area.
- Your legs get tired after a long day of work or play.
- You want to take your lower-body training to the next level.
- You avoid wearing shorts or anything that reveals your legs.
- You want to work on your whole body yet believe your legs could use a little extra help.

Keep the following points in mind as you begin the Lower-Body Focus Program.

- I have assigned the workouts to Monday, Tuesday, Thursday, and Friday of each week, but you can move your workouts to other days in the week if those are more convenient for you, or if you have more time to exercise on the weekend.
- The Lower-Body Focus Program consists of four workouts a week, with one workout each for the upper body and core and two workouts for the lower body. This means you get the benefits of a full-body workout with an extra lower-body workout to target your legs.
- Include a precision warmup for every workout by doing one easy circuit of the entire program to warm up your body for the specific routine ahead of you.
- Include a Precision Cardio workout two or three times a week. You can do your cardio workouts on the days you do your synergy set workouts or on your off days.
- Stay accountable by filling in your training logs. Be sure to record the number of reps or breaths you completed for each exercise or stretch. That way, you'll know what you need to do next time to continue to improve.
- When you're short on time or traveling, you can substitute an express workout.
- Remember that each workout requires an investment of 15 minutes or less. The days you can't find 15 minutes to do something positive for yourself are the days you deserve it most!

Lower-Body Focus: Basic Program

- Stay with the program a minimum of 6 weeks. After 6 weeks, you can repeat it or move on to the intermediate level.
- Remember that if an exercise is too challenging for you right now, you can do the beginner modification instead.
- Don't forget to stay hydrated as you work out. Be sure you have a water bottle nearby, and sip from it frequently.
- Include two or three Precision Cardio workouts per week.

Week	Monday	Tuesday	Wednesday	Thursday	Friday
1	Lower-Body Basics	Upper-Body Basics	—	Core Basics	Lower-Body Basics
2	Upper-Body Basics	Lower-Body Basics	—	Core Basics	Lower-Body Basics
3	Core Basics	Lower-Body Basics	—	Upper-Body Basics	Lower-Body Basics
4	Lower-Body Basics	Upper-Body Basics	—	Core Basics	Lower-Body Basics
5	Upper-Body Basics	Lower-Body Basics	—	Core Basics	Lower-Body Basics
6	Core Basics	Lower-Body Basics	—	Upper-Body Basics	Lower-Body Basics

Lower-Body Focus: Intermediate Program

- This program is the next level of the Lower-Body Focus Program.
- Stay with this plan for a minimum of 6 weeks. That will give you 12 lower-body workouts and 6 upper-body and core workouts.
- After 6 weeks, you can repeat the program or move on to the next level.
- Include two or three Precision Cardio workouts per week.
- Remember that each workout requires an investment of approximately 12 minutes. The days you can't find 12 minutes to work out are the days you should give yourself a half-hour!

Week	Monday	Tuesday	Wednesday	Thursday	Friday
1	Lower-Body Intermediate	Upper-Body Intermediate	—	Core Intermediate	Lower-Body Intermediate
2	Upper-Body Intermediate	Lower-Body Intermediate	—	Core Intermediate	Lower-Body Intermediate
3	Core Intermediate	Lower-Body Intermediate	—	Upper-Body Intermediate	Lower-Body Intermediate
4	Lower-Body Intermediate	Upper-Body Intermediate	—	Core Intermediate	Lower-Body Intermediate
5	Upper-Body Intermediate	Lower-Body Intermediate	—	Core Intermediate	Lower-Body Intermediate
6	Core Intermediate	Lower-Body Intermediate	—	Upper-Body Intermediate	Lower-Body Intermediate

LOWER-BODY FOCUS: CHALLENGE PROGRAM

- This program is the advanced level of the Lower-Body Focus Program.
- Stay with this plan for a minimum of 6 weeks. That will be 12 lower-body workouts and 6 upper-body and core workouts.
- Include two or three Precision Cardio workouts per week.

- Some of the exercises in these workouts may be particularly challenging. If they're too tough at first, try the beginner option that's offered for each exercise. As you progress, you can move from the easier options to the more challenging ones.

Week	Monday	Tuesday	Wednesday	Thursday	Friday
1	Lower-Body Challenge	Upper-Body Challenge	—	Core Challenge	Lower-Body Challenge
2	Upper-Body Challenge	Lower-Body Challenge	—	Core Challenge	Lower-Body Challenge
3	Core Challenge	Lower-Body Challenge	—	Upper-Body Challenge	Lower-Body Challenge
4	Lower-Body Challenge	Upper-Body Challenge	—	Core Challenge	Lower-Body Challenge
5	Upper-Body Challenge	Lower-Body Challenge	—	Core Challenge	Lower-Body Challenge
6	Core Challenge	Lower-Body Challenge	—	Upper-Body Challenge	Lower-Body Challenge

LOWER-BODY FOCUS: EXPRESS PROGRAM

- This program is for you if you want a quick and effective plan with a minimum of equipment.
- The express workouts can be done whenever you're pressed for time. Or you can use them in a 6-week program, as shown here.
- Include two or three Precision Cardio workouts per week.

Week	Monday	Tuesday	Wednesday	Thursday	Friday
1	Lower-Body Express	Upper-Body Express	—	Core Express	Lower-Body Express
2	Upper-Body Express	Lower-Body Express	—	Core Express	Lower-Body Express
3	Core Express	Lower-Body Express	—	Upper-Body Express	Lower-Body Express
4	Lower-Body Express	Upper-Body Express	—	Core Express	Lower-Body Express
5	Upper-Body Express	Lower-Body Express	—	Core Express	Lower-Body Express
6	Core Express	Lower-Body Express	—	Upper-Body Express	Lower-Body Express

The Upper-Body Focus Program

The Upper-Body Focus Program is for you if:

- You have always spent time on your lower body but have avoided training your upper body.
- You want to be stronger to be able to lift groceries or your children more easily.
- You want to take your upper-body training to the next level.
- You avoid wearing sleeveless shirts.
- You want to work on your whole body yet believe your upper body could use a little extra help.

Keep the following points in mind as you begin the Upper-Body Focus Program.

- I have assigned the workouts to Monday, Tuesday, Thursday, and Friday of each week, but you can move your workouts to other days in the week if those are more convenient for you, or if you have more time to exercise on the weekend.
- The Upper-Body Focus Program consists of four workouts a week, with one workout each for the lower body and core and two workouts for the upper body. You get the benefits of a full-body workout with an extra upper-body workout for beautiful arms and shoulders.
- Include a precision warmup for every workout by doing one easy circuit of the entire program to warm up your body for the specific routine ahead of you.
- Include a Precision Cardio workout two or three times a week. You can do your cardio workouts on the days you do your synergy set workouts or on your off days.
- Stay accountable by filling in your training logs. Be sure to record the number of reps or breaths you completed for each exercise or stretch. That way, you'll know what you need to do next time to continue to improve.
- Remember that each workout requires an investment of about 12 minutes. The days you can't find 12 minutes to work out are the days you should give yourself a half-hour!
- When you're short on time or traveling, you can substitute an express workout.

UPPER-BODY FOCUS: BASIC PROGRAM

- Stay with the program a minimum of 6 weeks. After 6 weeks, you can repeat it or move on to the intermediate level.
- Remember that if an exercise is too challenging for you right now, you can do the beginner modification instead.
- Don't forget to stay hydrated as you work out. Be sure you have a water bottle nearby, and sip from it frequently.
- Include two or three Precision Cardio workouts per week.

Week	Monday	Tuesday	Wednesday	Thursday	Friday
1	Upper-Body Basics	Lower-Body Basics	—	Core Basics	Upper-Body Basics
2	Lower-Body Basics	Upper-Body Basics	—	Core Basics	Upper-Body Basics
3	Core Basics	Upper-Body Basics	—	Lower-Body Basics	Upper-Body Basics
4	Upper-Body Basics	Lower-Body Basics	—	Core Basics	Upper-Body Basics
5	Lower-Body Basics	Upper-Body Basics	—	Core Basics	Upper-Body Basics
6	Core Basics	Upper-Body Basics	—	Lower-Body Basics	Upper-Body Basics

UPPER-BODY FOCUS: INTERMEDIATE PROGRAM

- This program is the next level of the Upper-Body Focus Program.
- Stay with this plan for a minimum of 6 weeks. That will give you 12 upper-body workouts and 6 lower-body and core workouts.
- After 6 weeks, you can repeat the program or move on to the next level.
- Include two or three Precision Cardio workouts per week.

Week	Monday	Tuesday	Wednesday	Thursday	Friday
1	Upper-Body Intermediate	Lower-Body Intermediate	—	Core Intermediate	Upper-Body Intermediate
2	Lower-Body Intermediate	Upper-Body Intermediate	—	Core Intermediate	Upper-Body Intermediate
3	Core Intermediate	Upper-Body Intermediate	—	Lower-Body Intermediate	Upper-Body Intermediate
4	Upper-Body Intermediate	Lower-Body Intermediate	—	Core Intermediate	Upper-Body Intermediate
5	Lower-Body Intermediate	Upper-Body Intermediate	—	Core Intermediate	Upper-Body Intermediate
6	Core Intermediate	Upper-Body Intermediate	—	Lower-Body Intermediate	Upper-Body Intermediate

UPPER-BODY FOCUS: CHALLENGE PROGRAM

- This program is the advanced level of the Upper-Body Focus Program.
- Stay with this plan for a minimum of 6 weeks. That will be 12 upper-body workouts and 6 lower-body and core workouts.
- Include two or three Precision Cardio workouts per week.

- Some of the exercises in these workouts may be particularly challenging. If they're too tough at first, try the beginner option that's offered for each exercise. As you progress, you can move from the easier options to the more challenging ones.

Week	Monday	Tuesday	Wednesday	Thursday	Friday
1	Upper-Body Challenge	Lower-Body Challenge	—	Core Challenge	Upper-Body Challenge
2	Lower-Body Challenge	Upper-Body Challenge	—	Core Challenge	Upper-Body Challenge
3	Core Challenge	Upper-Body Challenge	—	Lower-Body Challenge	Upper-Body Challenge
4	Upper-Body Challenge	Lower-Body Challenge	—	Core Challenge	Upper-Body Challenge
5	Lower-Body Challenge	Upper-Body Challenge	—	Core Challenge	Upper-Body Challenge
6	Core Challenge	Upper-Body Challenge	—	Lower-Body Challenge	Upper-Body Challenge

UPPER-BODY FOCUS: EXPRESS PROGRAM

- This program is for you if you want a quick and effective plan with a minimum of equipment.
- The express workouts can be done whenever you're pressed for time. Or you can use them in a 6-week program, as shown here.
- Include two or three Precision Cardio workouts per week.

Week	Monday	Tuesday	Wednesday	Thursday	Friday
1	Upper-Body Express	Lower-Body Express	—	Core Express	Upper-Body Express
2	Lower-Body Express	Upper-Body Express	—	Core Express	Upper-Body Express
3	Core Express	Upper-Body Express	—	Lower-Body Express	Upper-Body Express
4	Upper-Body Express	Lower-Body Express	—	Core Express	Upper-Body Express
5	Lower-Body Express	Upper-Body Express	—	Core Express	Upper-Body Express
6	Core Express	Upper-Body Express	—	Lower-Body Express	Upper-Body Express

PART FOUR

THE 6-WEEK
NUTRITION PROGRAM

FUELING THE JOURNEY

Whenever I speak with women about food, I hear the same recurring theme: Everyone is either on a diet or off a diet but going on one soon.

I've noticed that it's very rare that a woman feels a sense of ease about her food choices. And what we eat is often tied up with how we feel about ourselves. We pride ourselves on counting carbs, limiting fat grams, or giving up sugar. In fact, we talk more about what we *don't* eat than what we do eat. Yet despite the countless diets that have come and gone over the years, people are fatter than ever and obesity is on the rise, not just for us but also for our children. Something isn't working.

The problem with diets is that going off a diet is the next step after going on one. Diets set us up for failure: They hold us to impossibly high standards and don't allow room for individual taste preferences or schedules. As a result, when we "fall off" the diet wagon—as we inevitably will—we often end up feeling out of control, unable to resist the high-fat, high-calorie foods we know aren't good for us. And because dieting slows down the body's metabolism, we end up gaining weight more easily than we did before we started dieting. In fact, most dieters end up gaining back all the weight they lost—and often even more.

Mentally, going on and off diets can be devastating to your feeling of self-worth. To lose weight only to gain it back makes you feel like you have no control. Despite all of your hard work, you're left feeling like a failure.

Even worse, some extreme diets are downright unhealthy. Think about it: Does it really seem correct that you can eat bacon and sauces made with heavy cream and still be healthy? Does quick weight loss make sense when you gain it all

back? If your diet plan isn't something you would feel comfortable allowing your child to do, can it really be that healthy for you?

It's time to forget about dieting and start using common sense. In the beginning of this book, we discussed why no single exercise plan works for everyone. It's time to approach nutrition with this same sense of balance and respect for our individual needs. We need a plan based on practical strategies that we can apply to our everyday lives, a plan that will support—not hinder—our workouts. Fortunately, this isn't as hard as it might seem—and it's certainly easier than following some restrictive diet that was designed for the largest audience possible and doesn't take into account your unique challenges.

That's the key, a plan that works for you. A plan that *you* create with some commonsense strategies. A plan that is unique to you because it evolved as you integrated these strategies into your life one week at a time.

SIMPLE STRATEGIES, BIG RESULTS

Each week for the next 6 weeks, I'll ask you to try out a few new strategies for healthy, balanced eating. All of these strategies will be simple, and none of them will require a large investment of time or money. Whereas diets give you strict rules and menu plans you must follow, the strategies I'm offering you are tools for living. They are guidelines you can adapt to your life, rather than strict rules you must follow or everything is ruined.

As you gradually begin to incorporate these strategies into your life, you're going to start seeing some major benefits. You'll start to notice that you're feeling better—less tired, more alert, more *balanced*. Your workouts will benefit, too, as you give your body the fuel it needs to get the most out of each exercise. Plus, you'll lose weight without even focusing on that as your goal. And the small victories are the ones that will motivate you to keep going.

The best part of these strategies is that *you* decide which ones work for you. I'm not here to dictate what you can and cannot eat. A balanced approach to eating hands the responsibility for healthy decisions back to you. I just provide the map and some suggested routes; you are the designated driver. You are the one who will find the path that works best for you. And when it is *your* ride that *you* choose, you'll find it easier to stay on the path.

Of course, for the greatest benefit, I suggest you integrate all of the strategies you're about to learn into your life. But if you don't want to do them all, you don't have to sit in the back of the classroom. Even if after the 6 weeks you keep only four of the strategies, you still have gained four good tools for living. Unlike extreme diets, every aspect of this plan is not dependent on the other. If you decide not to stick with one change, your whole plan won't go astray. And you may even find yourself coming back to some strategies later on, when you realize they weren't as hard as the strict diet plans you used to follow that never worked anyway. Remember, this is your body, your pace, your plan: One size does *not* fit all.

Over the next 6 weeks, you'll be adding new actions and replacing unhealthy habits with positive ones. I'm not going to badger you to eliminate things; instead, I'd like you to approach each week with the goal of increasing positive habits. You'll be learning by doing. And with each small change you make, you'll notice a dramatic impact on your health, your weight, your workouts, and your mood. With this one-two punch of precision workouts and practical nutrition strategies, nothing can stop you from attaining the lean, long, and strong body you've always wanted.

This week's Strategies for Success are:

- ☐ Write down everything you eat and drink.
- ☐ Record the approximate amounts.
- ☐ Note the time of each meal or snack.
- ☐ Rate your hunger on a scale of 1 to 5.
- ☐ Rate your fullness on a scale of 1 to 5.
- ☐ Record how you feel at each meal or snack.

Information is power. The more you know about your habits, choices, and assumptions about your diet, the more control you have.

This week, I want you to track what you eat and drink by keeping a food journal. That's it! There are no other requirements. Don't worry about whether you're making "good" or "bad" food choices; you don't have to take away or change anything just yet. Simply eat the way you normally do and record everything in your food journal. Just increasing your awareness will remind you that you are in control of your food choices.

So many women wonder why they can't lose weight. Or they can't figure out how they put on a few pounds even though they were on a new diet plan. Too often we are unaware of what we're *really* eating throughout the day. We may forget about the midafternoon snacks we have each day, the bites of "this and that" we mindlessly eat as we prepare dinner, or the handful of pretzels we have while we watch TV.

It all comes down to common sense. We have to know what we're doing to figure out how we got there. Keeping a food journal is like turning on a light to finally see what's going on. The act of writing down what you eat each day puts you back in control and reinforces what is important to you.

Your food log won't look like anyone else's—and that's as it should be, since no one else is exactly like you. The information you glean from it will help you to figure out an individual plan that works for you. You'll uncover those unique eating patterns and habits that are sabotaging your efforts to be fit and healthy. Perhaps you'll find that after every stressful meeting with your supervisor, you head for the cookies. Or maybe you'll discover you're eating too late at night or most of your calories are coming from cappuccinos with whipped cream.

You are the director of your life, and your journal is a way to track the action. As you address problem behaviors and replace them with healthy alternatives, you'll notice that your energy level and feelings of well-being increase. And by turning up your awareness on what you eat throughout the day, you will jump-start your weight loss. Just paying attention causes us to listen to our bodies' signals. We start to wait until we are hungry to eat and stop when we first realize we've had enough. Dialing in and looking, really looking, at what you are eating is a commonsense strategy that is the basis for weight loss.

You're going to discover a lot of interesting things about yourself in just 1 week. But to get the full benefit of the journal, I'd like you to continue writing in it for a full 6 weeks. That way, you'll not only uncover unhealthy habits and patterns, but you'll be able to track your progress as you add in healthy actions to replace them.

GETTING STARTED: CHOOSE YOUR JOURNAL

First off, you'll need a notebook or journal that has at least 50 pages. It can be as simple as a spiral-bound notebook that you buy for around a dollar in a drugstore or grocery store, or as elegant as a beautifully bound journal with a fabric cover that you purchase in a card or gift store. The choice is yours; buy what works for you. Since you're going to be carrying it with you throughout the next few weeks, I do recommend choosing something that you can fit in your purse, briefcase, or book bag.

To keep things simple, I suggest making day one of your journal a Monday, which will make it easy to track the weeks. I also recommend that you record throughout the day so you won't forget anything. The best way to do this is to carry your journal with you, tucked in your purse or your pocket. If that's impossible, keep your journal in a place that you can easily get to throughout the day, such as your desk drawer or your locker. If your job has you on the road most days, you might want to keep your journal in the glove compartment of your car, so it's always with you. If you have no choice but to record at the end of the day, rather than throughout, make mental notes at each meal or snack.

As is the case with anything new, the first week keeping your journal will be the most challenging. But remember, for a small commitment of time and effort, you'll reap huge rewards!

RECORD EVERYTHING YOU EAT AND DRINK

Copy the columns that I have provided in the sample journal on page 264. Then start by simply recording everything you eat and drink on your first day. This includes all beverages from water to coffee.

Remember that no one is judging you on what you write in your journal. Arlene, a new client of mine, had a hard time with this. She would start her journal and then throw it away the next day if she had eaten something she considered "bad." She didn't want me to see her "bad" foods because she thought I'd take them away from her, so she resolved to start again the next day, eating only food she thought I'd like.

What was the secret she was trying to hide? Arlene had a tendency to eat too many cookies after her kids fell asleep. Contrary to popular belief, I am not the food police. I wasn't going to raid her cupboards in the middle of the night (and keep her homemade cookies for myself). It wasn't I who was going to make the final decisions about what she ate—that was up to Arlene. I was just going to help her uncover her unhealthy eating patterns and assist her in finding common-sense solutions.

By looking at Arlene's food log, we were able to figure out that she didn't eat enough during the day, which led to her late-night binges. That information helped her to plan to eat more throughout the day, so she could feel content with a small dessert after dinner, rather than emptying the kids' cookie jar late at night because she was starving. She simply needed to bring balance into her day.

To make informed decisions, you need *all* the information you can gather, so don't edit anything out. Just write it all down, even if it makes you cringe. Remember, information is power.

RECORD THE AMOUNTS OF FOOD YOU EAT

Leslie, another client of mine, was always tired and wasn't losing the weight she wanted to. Yet her food log showed that she was making healthy choices; in fact, she was eating the same foods that I eat. The problem was that she had neglected to record the amounts. When we discovered that she was eating enormous servings of certain foods, we made some adjustments. We cut down the large quantity of proteins and fats she was eating and increased her servings of vegetables and fruits. Now, instead of snacking on high-calorie nuts all day and having way too much protein at each meal, she snacks on fresh fruit and replaces half of her large serving of fish with vegetables at her evening meal.

Of course, few of us really know what a half cup of rice or 4 ounces of fish looks like. So for the first few days, I'd like you to measure out your food so you can be sure the amounts you record are accurate. Later on, when you have a better idea of what a serving size looks like, it will be fine to estimate. If you don't have a food scale, just divide the portions up. For example, if you buy a pound (16 ounces uncooked) of fish, you can cut it in half to make two 8-ounce portions, and in half again to make four 4-ounce portions.

NOTE THE TIME OF EACH MEAL OR SNACK

Do you bustle through your day, bouncing from one appointment or task to another, with barely time to even think about food? If so, you probably find yourself settling down to a huge dinner in the evening, when you're finally able to catch your breath. Schedules like these are common, and they mean that many of us tend to eat all or most of our calories in one part of the day, rather than spreading them throughout our waking hours. The problem with this is that food is the body's fuel, and when we're running low, it means that our energy suffers. As a result, we may get cranky and irritable, and slog through our day, wishing we could take a nap. As you record the time of each meal or snack, obvious patterns will emerge.

Another common challenge is the midafternoon slump. You may discover that every afternoon, you reach for a candy bar to last you until dinner. But by identifying this pattern, you can plan ahead to avoid it. Perhaps when you make your lunch in the morning, you can pack some additional healthy snacks, such as nuts or some fruit, so you don't become powerless to a vending machine.

Weekends can be particularly tricky. Often women will have a huge breakfast with their families on Saturday or Sunday morning, then skip lunch and dinner because they ate too many pancakes. But by late evening, they're starving, so they eat whatever's fast and easy, which could mean ice cream, cookies, or chips. If this is a problem for you, your food journal will help you recognize it.

RATE YOUR HUNGER ON A SCALE OF 1 TO 5

Very often, we don't even know for sure when we're hungry. We eat according to some previously determined schedule that has nothing to do with how we feel. For example, 9:00 A.M. means breakfast, 12 noon means lunch, and 7:00 P.M. means dinner. Hungry or not, that's when we've been told we're supposed to eat our meals.

Says who? What if you wake up at 5:00 A.M. every day? What if you're hungry at 10:00 A.M.—do you have to wait until the official lunchtime? Even if you can't take a full break at 10:00, can you have a small snack?

Instead of following some preset schedule created for the "average" person (and who is this Ms. Average? I haven't met an average person, ever!), try to tune in to your hunger and respond to that. I find that when women are truly hungry, they crave simple, healthy foods. A piece of fish and a salad will do. An apple is the perfect snack. Yet when are we truly hungry? We are bombarded with cues to eat all day long. Are we running to the local fast-food restaurant because of hunger, or due to their latest marketing campaign?

Learning to identify true hunger is a tool for getting off the diet roller coaster. Learning to eat when you're hungry and to stop eating when you're full is an essential commonsense strategy that will result in lasting changes. With that in mind, I'd like you to rate your hunger on a scale of 1 to 5 before each meal or snack you eat.

Hunger Rating
1: Uncomfortably full
2: Full; no feeling of hunger at all
3: Not hungry but not full
4: Hungry; would like to eat to satisfy hunger
5: Extremely hungry; stomach is growling

RATE YOUR FULLNESS FACTOR ON A SCALE OF 1 TO 5

Have you ever been so full you felt like you were going to explode? Well, blame your brain. Or, more specifically, the communication lines between your brain and your stomach. It takes about 15 to 20 minutes for our brains to realize that our stomachs are full. Yet in those 15 to 20 minutes, we can easily finish a second helping or polish off a rich dessert. So by the time we realize we're full, we've already eaten more than we need.

The key to recognizing fullness is to slow down as you eat. That way, you give your brain a chance to catch up to your stomach. As you learn to slow down at your meals, you'll learn to stop eating when you feel satisfied rather than when you feel uncomfortable. For this first week, though, I simply want you to be aware of your feelings of fullness. Remember: Awareness is the first step to lasting change.

Record in your journal the feeling of fullness you had when you finished eating each meal or snack.

Fullness Factor
1: Still very hungry
2: Not too hungry but still able to eat more
3: Satisfied; not too full
4: Had a little too much
5: Stuffed; extremely uncomfortable

RECORD YOUR FEELING FACTOR

Finally, I want you to ask yourself how you're feeling before you have each meal or snack. Are you bored? Tired? Nervous? Angry with your significant other or your boss? Jot it down in your journal. Even if it's just a one-word description, that's okay.

In the coming weeks, you'll probably see patterns emerge. Maybe you crave high-fat comfort foods like macaroni and cheese when you're feeling anxious. Or perhaps you head for the chips and dip when you're bored. Maybe you tend to overeat when you go to a big gathering, such as a party or holiday get-together.

There are many reasons why we eat, and why we choose the foods we do. You might be reaching for chocolate chip cookies because they made you feel better when you were a child. But I'd be willing to bet they don't have the same effect now that you're an adult. Why not? Well, perhaps life is more beautifully complex, and a cookie doesn't make it all better. Instead, it probably just leaves you feeling guilty for your indulgence—on top of whatever negative feelings you were trying to relieve.

And unfortunately, when you eat to relieve troubling feelings, you tend to overeat. It's as if you're stuffing down your anger or your stress or your fear along with the cookies. When you're upset, you turn off your awareness of what you're eating. As a result, you don't realize you're full until you've eaten much more than you normally would.

Medicating yourself with food doesn't solve anything. It doesn't make you feel better; it just postpones your feelings for a while. And then you feel worse about yourself, and it becomes an endless cycle. You can't erase feelings or stressful situations, but you can change how you deal with them. Instead of compounding the problem by overeating, you can learn to substitute healthier activities that really *do* make you feel better.

The first step is to recognize the cues—the feelings and thoughts that lead you to the kitchen, the vending machine, or the fast-food drive-thru. Once you've identified these cues, you can brainstorm alternative ways to deal with your feelings instead of eating. For example, I have a client who lies across her exercise ball and stretches her back when she feels stressed. On the other hand, a reader e-mailed me one day to tell me that she likes to go to my Web page and read the fitness tips there when she feels bored. Personally, I like to take a walk with my greyhound, Griffin (who used to live at a racetrack), to put life in perspective. If you need some help getting started, here's a quick list of some alternate activities you could try.

Feeling Factor	Alternate Action
Tired	Take a nap.
	Take a walk.
	Go to sleep for the night.
Stressed	Write in your journal.
	Call a friend.
	Do some stretches.
Anxious	Exercise.
	Take a bath.
	Clean the house.
Bored	Prepare meals for the next day.
	Exercise.
	Read a book that feeds your mind.
Lonely	Call a friend or family member.
	Write in your journal.
	Write a letter or e-mail to a friend.
Angry	Ask yourself what you're angry about and write it in your journal.
	Give yourself a pedicure.
Sad	Write in your journal about your sadness.
	Count the things in your life to be grateful for.
	Do your favorite weekend activity, like going for a bike ride.
Hungry	Eat a mindful meal and enjoy the experience.
	Ask yourself what you really need; if you still feel hungry, have a meal or snack.

Sample Food Journal

Here's a template to use when you begin your food journal. I recommend either photocopying this page or rewriting these columns in your notebook so that you won't forget to record any of the relevant information.

Week #

Day	Food Eaten (including amounts)	Time	Hunger Rating	Fullness Factor	Feeling Factor
MONDAY					
Meal 1:					
Meal 2:					
Meal 3:					
Snacks:					
TUESDAY					
Meal 1:					
Meal 2:					
Meal 3:					
Snacks:					
WEDNESDAY					
Meal 1:					
Meal 2:					
Meal 3:					
Snacks:					
THURSDAY					
Meal 1:					
Meal 2:					
Meal 3:					
Snacks:					
FRIDAY					
Meal 1:					
Meal 2:					
Meal 3:					
Snacks:					
SATURDAY					
Meal 1:					
Meal 2:					
Meal 3:					
Snacks:					
SUNDAY					
Meal 1:					
Meal 2:					
Meal 3:					
Snacks:					

This week's new Strategies for Success are:

☐ Increase your water intake, with the goal of drinking eight 8-ounce glasses each day.
☐ Choose foods in their purest state.

You'll also want to:

☐ Record Week 2 in your food journal.

Welcome to Week 2! In addition to continuing to write in your food journal, you will be learning two new strategies this week. Both are powerful, and I think you'll be surprised by the results you'll see at the end of the 7 days.

INCREASE THE AMOUNT OF WATER YOU DRINK

It's pretty easy to spot a houseplant that hasn't had enough water—it's parched, dry, and tired-looking. But as soon as you start to water it regularly, it seems to suddenly spring to life. In the same way, increasing your own water intake will help you blossom.

Think about it: Your body is made up of approximately 60 percent water. And your brain? Believe it or not, it's 75 percent water. Your body needs water for every task that it performs. From digestion to metabolism, water is essential. When you aren't taking in enough water, you simply can't perform at your best.

That's why this week, I'd like you to gradually increase your water intake, with the goal of working up to eight 8-ounce glasses of water a day. I realize this recommendation isn't new—you've probably heard it before, and maybe you've passed it off as something that's been around so long, it

can't be important. Yet it's amazing what a difference such a simple change can make. When you're not properly hydrated, it's like trying to go about your day with one hand tied behind your back. Sure, you can survive, but you're certainly not functioning at your best. But when you give your body the water it needs, you're unleashing its abilities to work as the finely tuned, efficient machine it is. Your digestive system will work better, you'll be able to think more clearly, your metabolism will become more efficient, your skin will look better, and you'll feel fuller longer.

And speaking of feeling full, many of us who don't get enough water are mistaking our bodies' pleas for fluid as pleas for food. In other words, we think we're hungry when we're merely thirsty. Talk about a waste of calories! Instead of a snack, a cold glass of water will often do the trick. Plus, drinking water is a natural energy booster: Feeling tired is a common, though often unrecognized, symptom of dehydration.

If you're not used to drinking water frequently throughout the day, eight glasses can seem like a lot. So give yourself a couple of days to work up to that; for your first day, try getting at least four glasses of water, then add a glass each day until you're up to eight. And be sure to space the glasses out throughout the day so you don't get stuck with drinking them all at night. By slowly integrating drinking more water into your daily routine, you'll improve your chances of it becoming part of your daily life. Eventually, downing eight glasses a day will become a no-brainer.

Smart Sipping Strategies

If you're wondering how on earth you're going to drink 64 ounces—yes, that's a half gallon, or

2 quarts—of water each day, check out the following strategies.

Put a big glass of water on your bedside table. That way, you can take a few sips before you go to sleep and if you wake up during the night. Of course, if your cat knocks it over like mine does, you might want to use a nonbreakable bottle instead of a glass.

Have a glass of water while you're preparing your meals. A good rule is to finish the glass you're drinking before you sit down to eat.

Have a bottle of water during your workout. Some readers have told me that they can't drink while they're working out, because it makes them feel nauseated. If you have the same problem, remember that you don't have to drink a lot. Just try to get yourself used to taking in a bit of water. If you're really struggling, you might even try just going through the motion of drinking: Put the water bottle up to your mouth, and pour out a few drops. You may be surprised how good the water tastes. Before long, your system will get used to it, and you'll be able to drink more.

Substitute water for fruit juice. Besides adding to your water intake, you'll be taking away the extra calories and sugar from fruit juice. If you want orange juice, eat an orange with its fiber intact. A medium orange is about 62 calories with 3.14 grams of filling fiber. A glass of orange juice is 113 calories with almost no fiber. When you want to drink something, drink water. Add a slice of orange as a garnish.

Think pure instead of highly processed. Wondering what I mean by a "highly processed" beverage? Just read the label on the next soda or iced tea you come across. There are some great drinks from responsible companies, but the majority of commercial beverages have ingredients in them that should not be going into your body on a regular basis. Drink water instead. If increasing your water intake means one less sugary soda a day or a smaller coffee drink, you're doing something positive for yourself. And that's what this week and every week is all about.

Carry a bottle of water with you. Drink from it during your commute to and from work and while you run errands.

Do We Need a Coffee Break or Just a Break?

Caramel swirl lattes. French vanilla cappuccinos. Nowadays, taking a coffee break can be more like taking a dessert break.

If you've gotten into the habit of regularly indulging in coffee drinks that contain loads of sugar and whipped cream (not to mention up to 300 calories), next time try substituting a glass of water and a cup of tea instead of your usual coffee drink. After all, what you need is a break, not whipped cream and sugar.

If you really want coffee, go ahead and have it. But stick with the traditional, no-frills kind— that means no whipped cream or sugary flavorings—with a little fat-free or soy milk. And along with the coffee, have a glass of water. The water will help fill you up, which means your coffee break won't turn into a coffee and doughnut break. Plus, you'll feel more energized because you'll avoid the sugar highs and lows of your former high-octane coffee drink.

Keep a bottle of water on your desk. Make a point of sipping from it throughout the day. And if you attend a lot of meetings, take it with you. When it's on the table in front of you, you'll probably keep sipping from it without even thinking about it.

Perk it up. If you don't like the taste of water, try adding a slice of orange, lime, or lemon. Or add a splash of cranberry juice for a refreshing treat. You can even try sparkling water or seltzer. Most stores carry a great selection of flavored bottled waters; just check the label to make sure there is no added sugar or chemicals in the brand you're considering buying. Or try my trick: Buy some plain mineral water and then add a strawberry or a few raspberries for a homemade flavored drink.

Drink before you order. If you're out at a restaurant, have a glass of water before you order your food. You will be less hungry and able to make better choices from the menu.

Eat Closer to the Source

In addition to drinking more water this week, I also want you to make a conscious effort to eat closer to the source. Simply put, this means eating foods in their purest, most natural state. When you're deciding whether or not to eat something, ask yourself, "Where did this food come from?" If you can't figure out how it got from the tree or farm to your plate, it probably picked up a lot of sugar, fat, and chemicals along the way.

If a food didn't exist a thousand years ago, if it doesn't resemble anything that comes off a tree or out of a farm, then it's probably not your healthiest choice. In later weeks, we'll be refining this strategy even further as we look specifically at carbohydrates, proteins, and fats. But as an overall plan for healthful eating and quick results, this strategy can't be beat.

I'm not asking you to give up all the foods you've been eating, but I do want you to consider the differences between foods that are closer to the source and those that are farther away. Here, at a glance, is how they compare, nutrition-wise.

Closer to the Source	Farther from the Source
Higher water content	Lower water content
Fewer preservatives	More preservatives
More fiber	Less fiber
Fewer calories	More calories
Greater amounts and higher quality of vitamins and minerals	Fewer and lower-quality vitamins and minerals

As an added bonus, because foods closer to the source have a higher fiber content, you need less to feel full. Think about it: When was the last time you ate too many apples? But eating too much apple pie is easy. For the number of calories in just one slice of pie, you could have had more than four apples with more fiber and no saturated fat.

	Apple	Apple Pie
Amount	1 medium	1 small slice
Calories	80	355
Total Fat	0.4 g	16.5 g (4.5 g saturated fat)
Dietary Fiber	3.7 g	2.4 g

Of course, eating closer to the source isn't limited to choosing a piece of fruit over a slice of pie. Consider the following comparison between a baked potato and its cousin, the french fry.

	Baked Potato	Curly French Fries
Amount	1 medium	1 cup
Calories	115	275
Total Fat	0.05 g	14.8 g (3.2 g saturated fat)
Sodium	12.2 mg	159.8 mg
Dietary Fiber	4.6 g	2.8 g

As you plan your meals this week, try to replace highly processed foods with those closer to the source. And make a point of reading the label on any packaged food you buy. You might be surprised to discover that sometimes, the food that the product is supposed to be based on isn't even listed among the first few ingredients!

Here are a few ideas to get you started with your substitutions.

Closer to the Source	Away from the Source
Peanut butter	Peanut butter cups
Broiled fish	Fried fish cakes
Bananas	Banana cream pie
Orange	Orange drink
Whole grain cereal	Sugared cereal
Whole grain bread	White bread
Blueberries and whole grains	Blueberry muffin
Baked potato	Potato chips
Low-fat cheese	Cheese puffs
A handful of raisins	Chocolate bar
Sliced turkey breast	Processed chicken roll
Sliced lean roast beef	Bologna
Yogurt	Protein bar
All-Bran with fat-free milk	Fat-free bran muffin
Salad with sun-dried tomatoes and avocado	Salad with croutons and bacon bits
Whole grain cracker	Doughnut
Peach	Canned peaches in syrup
Steamed spinach with lemon	Creamed spinach
Frozen grapes	Ice cream

Week 3: Become Carb Savvy

This week's new Strategies for Success are:

☐ Eat at least four servings of smart carbs each day.

☐ Limit conscious carbs to two or three servings a day, and stay aware of portion size.

☐ Have one or two servings of fruit each day.

You'll also want to:

☐ Record Week 3 in your food journal.

☐ Drink at least eight 8-ounce glasses of water each day.

☐ Eat closer to the source.

Last week, we discussed the health benefits of eating closer to the source. This week, we're going to take that goal one step further. Over the next 7 days, I'd like you to concentrate on increasing the amount of smart carbs you eat.

Lately, "carbohydrate" has become a dirty word. It seems that everywhere we turn, someone is on a low-carb diet. All of a sudden, carbohydrates have become the enemy, and bacon is being embraced as a smart choice. There's something wrong with that picture.

So what are smart carbs, and why in the world would I want you to eat *more* of them?

Simply put, smart carbs are vegetables. And despite what you might have heard, they are the ultimate food for becoming lean, long, and strong: They're full of nutrients, low in calories, and high in fiber. As a bonus, the fiber and water in vegetables fill you up quickly, so you'll be satisfied sooner.

With all the good things vegetables do for you, it's amazing to find that many people go for days without eating any vegetables at all. French fries don't count! Neither does ketchup or the tomato sauce on a slice of pizza.

This week, try to have at least four servings of vegetables each day. (A serving is about 1 cup of raw vegetables.) After increasing the number of veggies you eat, I think you'll be surprised how much better you feel at week's end. And even though I'm asking you only to increase your servings of smart carbs, when you do, I think you'll find that you naturally decrease the number of processed foods you consume. And that is one very big bonus.

SMART CARBS VERSUS NO CARBS

Recently, I was in the grocery store and saw a woman who had just joined the gym where I train my clients. She was loading up on low-carb bars. As soon as she saw me, her eyes went to my grocery cart. This happens all the time, as if what I put in my cart holds the secret for a fit body. "All those carbs," she commented, as she scanned the pineapples, bunches of greens, and bags of peppers and tomatoes that were overflowing my cart. "How do you stay so lean if you eat all those carbs?"

Let me say it loud and clear: Carbs are not evil. In fact, they're the body's main source of energy. And despite what advocates of some diet fads might have you believe, it isn't the carbs in vegetables and fruits that you need to watch out for. It's the overly processed carbs in foods such as cookies and cake that cause cravings and pile on the calories. *Those* are the carbs we need to avoid to feel our best.

As for my friend in the grocery store, I think she, like many others, has become the victim of some clever marketing strategies. The low-carb food craze that has hit grocery stores reminds me of the fat-free food craze of a few years ago. The underlying motive is the same: Food companies need to keep selling their products, most of which are highly processed. So they take out something in a food product that people are convinced is making them fat (carbs or fat) and replace it with something else, which usually ends up being something that will still make them fat.

Think about it: Can carb-free cookies really be the best choices for long-term health and weight control? Products like these just make you want more. One cookie leads to two, because they don't satisfy you nutritionally. That leads to more cravings, a decrease in energy, and weight gain. Wouldn't you be better off having a couple of apples—carbs and all—with the fiber and nutrients intact?

Last week, we talked about eating closer to the source. Perhaps no better example exists of why this is important than when you consider carb-free foods. These foods were created by scientists who took out the carbs and added fat and a bunch of laboratory-made substances that our bodies just don't know what to do with. Which is a better choice for lunch, a chocolate coconut low-carb bar that has been sitting on a shelf for months or a big bowl of vegetable stir-fry? Take a look at the comparison below and then ask yourself which ingredients you want in your body.

Tips to Become a Veteran Veggie Eater

As you increase your vegetable intake, you'll find yourself naturally eating fewer highly processed foods. You simply won't have room for them, because you'll be getting full from the fiber and water content of the vegetables. That means this one easy strategy will pay off with double dividends. To start reaping the rewards of a veggie-rich diet, try the following tips, which will help you easily incorporate more smart carbs into your meals and snacks.

Be careful how your vegetables are prepared. Fresh is best. Go for steamed or lightly sautéed instead of creamed or fried. And instead of adding butter or cheese, try a squirt of fresh lemon juice or a bit of garlic.

Become salad savvy. Salads are great as long as you don't top them with high-fat dressings. When dining out, always order the dressing on the side so you have control over the amount you use. And choose a light vinaigrette or olive oil and vinegar instead of heavy cheese- or cream-based dressings.

Have a salad with your meal. The water content of the vegetables will fill you up, so you'll

	Vegetable Stir-Fry	Chocolate Coconut Low-Carb Bar
Amount	1 cup	1 bar
Calories	117	250
Protein	5 g	18 g
Carbs	25 g	2 g
Fat	0.6 g	13 g
Ingredients	Corn, green beans, lima beans, squash, red and green peppers, cauliflower, mushrooms, onions, peas, soy sauce, vinegar	Isolated soy protein, glycerine, polydextrose (Litesse), water, whey protein isolate, natural palm kernel oil, lecithin, calcium/sodium caseinate, ghee (clarified butter), natural coconut oil, high oleic sunflower oil, coconut, cocoa, natural flavors, potassium citrate, potassium chloride, citric acid, sucralose (a nonnutritive sweetener), potassium sorbate, and the following vitamins and minerals: tricalcium phosphate, calcium carbonate, magnesium oxide, vitamin A, vitamin C, vitamin D_3, thiamin, riboflavin, pyridoxine, cyanocobalamin, vitamin E acetate, niacin, biotin, pantothenic acid, copper, zinc, iodine, folic acid, chromium chelate

be satisfied with a smaller entrée and have an easier time saying no to dessert.

Buy bags of prewashed greens for salads at home. With these, throwing a salad together takes just minutes. Simply add tomatoes, cucumbers, peppers, or any other fresh vegetable you can think of.

Don't forget the frozen foods aisle. With frozen vegetables, you have almost no prep work, and you don't need to worry about using up the vegetables in a certain amount of time before they spoil. So stock your freezer with a variety of frozen veggies, which you can use straight or add to your favorite soup. Good vegetables for soup-making include string beans and carrots. You can even sprinkle a handful of frozen peas onto your salad for a delicious crunch.

Heat up a stir-fry. Here's another use for frozen veggies: Pour a bag of premixed frozen vegetables into a nonstick skillet or wok, add a little low-sodium soy sauce, and presto—you've got a fast and easy stir-fry. You can add a little olive oil and garlic for extra flavor.

Follow the two-to-one rule. Whenever you eat protein, such as fish, chicken, or red meat, make sure you have some vegetables with it. If there is a serving of protein on your plate, the amount of vegetables should be twice as much. (More on this in Week 5.)

Experiment with vegetables you have never tried. This week, make a point of trying at least two types of vegetables you've never eaten before or ones you've tasted at a restaurant but never prepared at home. Look in the produce section of your grocery store to see what's in season and looking fresh. For example, sugar snap peas, fresh from the store, make a great snack when you want to munch on something crunchy and sweet.

My absolute favorite item to add to a salad is a handful of grape tomatoes, which are even smaller than cherry tomatoes. If you haven't tried them yet, check them out. Another way to liven up a traditional salad is to toss in some kale, which is a great nutrient-rich green. I also love to steam kale and eat it plain as a side dish. To create a sweet coleslaw, simply shred some carrots and cabbage and mix them with a little olive oil and vinegar. And the next time you're grilling fish or meat, try throwing some vegetables on the grill. Zucchini and peppers with a bit of olive oil and garlic are especially good. Or try roasting brussels sprouts in the oven with a little olive oil and pepper.

Make veggie wraps for an easy lunch. Take a few large romaine lettuce leaves and place some turkey breast or tuna fish in the center. Layer on slices of tomato, shredded greens, and some sprouts. Instead of heavy dressing, try a few thin slices of avocado. Roll it up and you've got a great meal to go.

Listen to your mother. When you were a child and wanted dessert, I'll bet your mom told you to "finish your vegetables first." Now that you're an adult, that's still a good rule to follow. Don't let a sweet replace one of your servings of vegetables. Ask yourself: "If I'm not hungry enough to finish my salad, do I really need dessert?"

CONSCIOUS CARBS: WHAT ROLE SHOULD GRAINS HAVE IN YOUR DIET?

Of course, vegetables aren't the only foods that are considered high in carbohydrates. Grains and foods made with grains, such as oatmeal, brown rice, and whole grain breads and cereals, also are prime sources of carbohydrates, and they can be part of a balanced diet. Potatoes and beans fall into this category, too. Not only do these foods provide energy, but they're a good source of iron and B vitamins. The problem is that they're calorically dense, and they don't have the water and fiber content of most vegetables, so you don't feel as full as fast. As a result, most women tend to eat too much of them. For this reason, I like to think of foods such as these as "conscious carbs." Sure you can eat them; just be aware of your serving size.

For example, it's pretty hard to eat too much broccoli. A cup or two, and you're usually satisfied. Yet 2 or 3 cups of rice can go down pretty quickly, especially if you haven't had any vegetables with it. And along with that rice come a lot of extra calories. Consider the following comparison.

	Cooked Broccoli	Brown Rice
Amount	1 cup	1 cup
Calories	44	216
Fiber	4.5 g	3.5 g

Try to have no more than one serving of conscious carbs at each meal. (A serving is ½ cup whole grain cereal or oatmeal, ½ cup rice, a slice of whole grain bread or one whole grain tortilla, two large whole grain crackers, one medium-size potato, or ½ cup beans.) If you tend to overeat conscious carbs, limit your portions by measuring the amount you eat. If you find that this just leaves you wanting more, and you'd prefer to eliminate them from your plan, make sure you double up on vegetables. The key is common sense and moderation. Again, one size does not fit all.

A good trick is to have small amounts of your conscious carbs early in the day, such as oatmeal in the morning and ½ cup rice with your lunch. This gives you plenty of time to use up the energy they provide.

A WORD ON FRUIT: NATURE'S DESSERT

Fruit falls right between the smart carbs I'd like you to increase and the conscious carbs I want you to limit. Fruits are amazing foods: Relatively low

Carbs at a Glance

From vegetables to grains to fruit to processed foods, there's a lot to know about carbs. But once you start paying attention to them, you'll find that you have more energy, lose weight more easily, and just plain feel better. Here, at a glance, are my guidelines for the carb-savvy eater.

Type of Carbohydrate	Servings per Day	Includes . . .
Smart carbs	At least 4	All fresh vegetables, frozen vegetables (excluding potatoes and those in heavy sauces)
Conscious carbs	No more than 2 or 3	Whole grains, beans, brown rice, oatmeal, whole grain breads and cereals, whole wheat pasta
Nature's desserts	1 or 2	All fresh fruit (try to stay away from dried fruit, which has all of the sugar and none of the water)
Processed carbs	Try to avoid; eat smart carbs instead.	Bread, cookies, muffins, pasta, any overly processed food

in calories, they're filled with fiber and nutrients, including carbs. They're the best desserts you can give yourself. Yet look to your food journal: If you tend to eat too many sweet fruits, such as bananas and dates, try substituting some high-water fruits such as apples, oranges, and melon. The challenge with sweet fruits such as dates and bananas is that they are high in sugar and low in water, so they add on calories and don't fill you up as much as the higher-water fruits do. A few dates or a banana as a treat is fine; just don't overdo it.

I've found that the women who consider fruit a forbidden food tend to binge on highly processed food. Denying themselves an apple or an orange just doesn't make sense if they wind up eating a bag of cookies. So if you haven't been eating fruit, try having one or two servings a day. I'll bet your cravings for processed sweets will disappear.

Finally, try to eat fruit as it came off the tree or vine, fresh and unprocessed. A great snack can be a bowl of watermelon, a cut-up apple, a pear, or some fresh pineapple. And the ultimate dessert is a bowl of frozen grapes or some slightly thawed berries. Freeze them for a few hours or more and then let them sit out for 15 minutes. The result is a delicious frozen treat, and unlike other frozen desserts, you'll actually know what the ingredients are in this one!

Week 4: Increase Healthy Fats

This week, I'd like you to concentrate on the following key Strategy for Success:

☐ Get one or two servings of healthy fats each day.

You'll also want to:

☐ Record Week 4 in your food journal.
☐ Drink eight 8-ounce glasses of water each day.
☐ Eat closer to the source.
☐ Eat four servings of smart carbs each day.
☐ Limit your servings of conscious carbs to three a day.
☐ Have one or two servings of fruit each day.

If there's one thing I want you to take away from this week, it's that *fat is not the enemy*. Unless you've been living in a cave somewhere, I'm sure you've heard the news that a low-fat diet reduces your risk for heart disease, stroke, and a host of other illnesses. Plus, it's one of the most highly touted strategies for weight loss. So all you need to do is limit all fats, and you're on your way to weight loss and good health—simple, right?

Not so fast. Somewhere along the way, the message about fats got a bit twisted. You see, like a lot of things, not *all* fats are bad. Some are actually quite good for you—for example, monounsaturated fats, such as those in olive and canola oils, may help lower the "bad" cholesterol (LDL) in your blood while increasing the "good" cholesterol (HDL). And the omega-3 fatty acids found in flaxseed and in fish such as salmon, herring, and mackerel can reduce blood pressure and may help decrease the risk of heart disease.

Meanwhile, a lot of the processed food advertised as "fat-free" or "low-fat" is anything but healthy, as we'll soon see.

HOW "FAT-FREE" MADE PEOPLE FATTER

When the "fat-free" craze hit the nation, food manufacturers got scared that there would be a dramatic drop in the sales of their high-fat products. So they reengineered many of these products to make them fat-free. But in place of the fat, they added additional sugar and, sometimes, unrecognizable ingredients to enhance the flavor and texture. Voilà! Fat-free cookies, muffins, potato chips, and ice cream.

Of course, all we had to do to find a naturally low-fat food was look in the produce section for a delicious array of fruits and vegetables. But why do that when we could eat fat-free cookies instead?

Yet fat-free cookies weren't very satisfying, so everyone would eat huge amounts of them. Plus, there's something about seeing the words *fat-free* on the label. It seems to give us license to eat. There we were, feeling virtuous for eating a fat-free version of a food that already lacked any nutritional value, and now was pumped up with additional sugar. We had cut out fats—both the good and the bad—and it was making us *fatter!*

Soon, the word got out that all this additional sugar was making us fat. Since sugar is a carbohydrate, it wasn't long before carbs became Public Enemy #1. We were told to go ahead and increase our fats, but to limit or avoid carbs. The problem was, which fats should we eat? This is where the extreme diets got really bizarre: We were told that it was okay to have bacon for breakfast, blue cheese on our burger for lunch, and a nice big steak for dinner. Just don't go near an orange!

Indigestion, anyone?

The Truth about Fat

It's time for a commonsense approach to fats. And this is one time when the "good" and "bad" categories are pretty clear-cut.

Bad fats. Saturated fats and trans fats are the prime offenders. Saturated fats are found in fatty meats such as beef, lamb, and pork (the marbling you see in these meats is pure saturated fat); full-fat dairy products such as whole milk, cream, butter, and full-fat cheeses; and palm kernel and coconut oils. Trans fats are the worst; they're found in margarine and vegetable shortening as well as packaged foods that use these ingredients, such as cookies, crackers, and pastries. They're also found in significant amounts in foods that have been deep-fried.

Good fats. Your body requires a small amount of "good" fat to function properly. We need fat for energy and to absorb fat-soluble vitamins such as A, D, E, and K. The trick is not to consume too much. A spoonful of olive oil on your salad, a handful of nuts, and a 4-ounce serving of salmon or tuna for dinner a few times a week are good ways to start increasing healthy fats. As you increase your healthy fats, you can easily reduce the unhealthy ones. For example, if you substitute fish or other seafood for red meat a few times a week, you get a double bonus: You've done something good for yourself by eating the fish while eliminating the saturated fat of the red meat.

A great additional benefit of these good fats is that they fill you up and keep you full longer. As the week progresses, you'll probably find yourself more satisfied with your meals, which will help stop the tendency to overeat or binge.

Here, at a glance, are the good fats. Try working in one or two servings of these a day.

- Oils: olive oil, canola oil, flaxseed oil, walnut oil
- Avocado
- Fish: salmon, tuna, mackerel, herring, sardines, and trout (Limit your serving size to 4 ounces uncooked.)
- Nuts: almonds, macadamia nuts, walnuts, Brazil nuts, pecans, and pistachios (Just be sure to stay aware of portion size; a serving of nuts should be no more than a handful. For natural nut butters, a spoonful goes a long way.)

Fast Tips to Increase Good Fats

Throughout the week, try a few of the following tips, which will make it easy to add good fats to your meals.

Think avocado, not cheese. Instead of heavy cheese, add a few pieces of avocado to your salad. You'll get that same rich taste, but it will come from monounsaturated fat, which can increase your levels of healthful, HDL cholesterol. Plus, avocados are rich in folate, vitamin E, potassium, iron, and magnesium.

Switch up your steak. Got the urge to sink your teeth into a steak? Make it a tuna steak instead of your usual T-bone.

Go nutty. A handful of nuts with a salad will turn a bowl of greens into a meal.

Toss some veggies with flaxseed oil. You can sneak some flaxseed oil into your diet by using it as a substitute for other vegetable oils when you make salad dressings.

Spoon on some flaxseed. High in fiber, flaxseed is also a rich source of lignans, hormones that may inhibit breast cancer. The easiest way to try it is to sprinkle a tablespoon or two on your cereal or in your juice. And if you enjoy baking, you can find delicious recipes in cookbooks and on Internet recipe databases for breads made with flaxseed.

Have a sweet treat on the run. A dab of almond butter on a sliced apple is so delicious it's almost decadent. The fat and protein in the almond butter fill you up, and the apple gives you energy to be lean, long, and strong.

Try some "bugs on a log." Spread some almond butter on a celery stalk. Dot with a few toasted sesame seeds. This snack is tasty, filling, and *great* for kids.

Discover that homemade dressing tastes best. In a blender, combine a few slices of avocado, some lemon juice, fresh garlic, and a dash of flaxseed or olive oil. This rich dressing beats any bottled dressing hands down.

Mix up some celery walnut rolls. Mix four stalks of sliced celery with some chopped green onion, chopped tomato, and a handful of chopped walnuts. For a dressing, squeeze the juice of half of an orange over the mixture. Roll up the mixture in romaine lettuce leaves or nori sheets. (Nori is a sea vegetable you can get in the Asian section of most supermarkets.)

Go for a Mediterranean dip. Mash chickpeas with tahini (a sesame seed butter that is a source of good omega fats) and fresh garlic. Use it as a dip for sliced peppers and zucchini.

Week 5: Get Practical about Protein

This week's Strategy for Success is:

☐ Eat 8 to 12 ounces of quality protein per day.

You'll also want to:

☐ Complete Week 5 of your food journal.
☐ Continue drinking eight glasses of water a day.
☐ Choose foods that are closer to the source.
☐ Eat at least four servings of smart carbs each day, and limit conscious carbs to three servings per day.
☐ Have one or two servings of fruit each day.
☐ Eat one or two servings of healthy fats per day.

Protein is essential for a strong body. You need it to maintain and repair your muscles, and it helps in the formation of hormones and enzymes that control your metabolism. If you don't have enough protein, your body starts to lose its muscle. Have you ever seen someone who is "skinny-fat"? Even though they're slim, their body lacks definition—they have no muscle tone. To support your workouts and get the sculpted body you want, you need appropriate amounts of protein.

When it comes to getting practical about protein, there are two issues to keep in mind: portion control and quality of protein. This week, you'll be working on both.

STRIKING A BALANCE BETWEEN TOO MUCH AND TOO LITTLE

Despite the important role protein plays in our bodies, there are still some women who don't get enough. They live on muffins for breakfast, a salad for lunch, and a plate of pasta for dinner.

There's just not enough protein there to maintain a healthy, sculpted body.

Elisabeth was a wonderful client of mine who trained consistently with the Lean, Long, and Strong workouts. Yet she wasn't seeing the definition in her body that she thought she should. When we discussed her diet, I discovered she wasn't eating any protein. In fact, she hadn't eaten protein in years, and she was hesitant to add too much into her diet. She was sure that the fat in protein would make her fat, and she never liked the taste of red meat or chicken. I was able to convince her to add two servings of fish each week, some tofu to her daily salads, and a handful of almonds to her morning serving of fruit. Not only did her muscle definition increase, but she felt stronger and less hungry throughout the day.

On the other hand, there are plenty of men and women who are on high-protein diets. They eat bacon with eggs for breakfast, a burger for lunch, and a steak or big piece of chicken for dinner. Sure, they're getting protein—but they're eating it at the expense of other food groups. And such large quantities of protein *aren't* a good thing.

Your body can't use more protein than it needs, so a high-protein diet translates into extra calories and weight gain. For most women, 4 to 6 ounces of protein at one meal should be enough, with no more than 8 to 12 ounces per day. Focus on having three servings a day of protein, which might include a cup of low-fat yogurt or 4 ounces of fish, lean poultry, or lean beef.

During the first few days of Week 1, you measured out your portions so you could visualize what a serving looks like. If you've forgotten what 4 ounces of protein looks like, it's a good idea to give yourself another quick lesson. I've found that one of the easiest ways to do this with meat and fish is to buy a pound and then divide it into four equal servings, which will leave you with perfect 4-ounce portions (uncooked weight). Or, perhaps easiest of all: A 4-ounce serving of meat or poultry is about the size of a deck of cards or the palm of your hand. And a serving of cottage cheese would fit in a cupped hand.

QUALITY COUNTS

Of course, the *quality* of the protein you choose can make a big difference. The key is to get your protein without consuming a lot of saturated fat in the process. So instead of a heavily marbled steak, choose a leaner cut, such as flank steak or filet mignon. And instead of high-fat cheeses, look for a low-fat replacement such as low-fat cottage cheese.

Other good sources of high-quality protein include fish; skinless chicken breast; skinless turkey breast; lean meat; egg whites; low-fat versions of yogurt, cheese, and other dairy products; beans; and soy.

When choosing what types of protein to have, use what you learned earlier about the benefits of eating closer to the source. For example, pick lean turkey breast instead of processed lunchmeat. And rather than highly processed and high-fat breakfast meats, try choosing a lean turkey patty or soy product instead. You may not even notice the difference!

The Two-to-One Rule

Years ago, I used to eat huge amounts of protein. I guess it was a result of being around lots of male bodybuilders in the gym. "Eat more protein," they would say in answer to everything.

"You want to get stronger? Eat more protein."

"You want to get leaner? Eat more protein."

"You want to learn to drive a stick shift? Eat more protein."

Yes, for them, protein was the answer to all of life's challenges.

So there I was, eating 12 egg whites at a time. I'd down a pound of turkey breast from the deli in minutes. I'd eat two cans of tuna in between classes—even though they'd smell up my book bag all day. Yet all that protein I was eating wasn't helping me get stronger, leaner, or even drive a stick shift. Driving a stick shift in New York City wasn't a priority. But I did want to get leaner, and what those guys were telling me wasn't working.

When it came time for my first bodybuilding competition, I used common sense. I looked at the amount of calories I was eating from protein and saw that it was way too much. So I devised a plan for myself: I could still eat protein, but whenever I had protein, I had to eat twice as many vegetables. If I wanted more protein after that, I had to eat vegetables with it.

Instead of 12 egg whites for breakfast, I would have 4 egg whites in an omelette with a lot of spinach. Instead of a whole pound of turkey breast sliced up from the deli, I would get 4 ounces and mix it into a huge salad. And instead of eating tuna straight from the can, which is what most bodybuilders ate in those days, I would mix the tuna with onions, tomatoes, and greens. I felt better and got leaner. That was more than 10 years ago, and I still live by the twice-as-many-vegetables-as-protein principle. It's healthy, it's practical, and it supports your workouts, helping you become lean, long, and strong.

Week 6: Become a Mindful Eater and Plan for Success

This week, your Strategies for Success are:

☐ Become a more mindful eater.
☐ Use your food journal to develop a daily plan that works best for you.

You'll also want to:

☐ Complete Week 6 of your food journal.
☐ Continue drinking at least eight glasses of water each day.
☐ Choose foods that are closer to the source.
☐ Eat at least four servings of smart carbs and no more than two or three servings of conscious carbs per day.
☐ Have one or two servings of fruit each day.
☐ Eat one or two servings of healthy fats per day.
☐ Eat 8 to 12 ounces of quality protein each day.

If you've been consistently trying out some of the previous week's strategies, by now, you should be seeing some positive results. You have gradually increased your healthy food habits and decreased your unhealthy ones. You've learned some broad-based strategies for making changes in your diet that can be customized to work for you, meeting your individual needs, taste preferences, and goals. I hope by now you understand why rigid diets don't work—and why they aren't even necessary. This week, we're going to take the basic strategies you've already learned and apply them. This week isn't so much about what you eat as how and why you eat and make certain food choices.

This week, there are two main goals: learning to become a more mindful eater and developing a daily plan for success.

STAYING AWARE, STAYING HEALTHY

Even when we've figured out what foods work best for us, making us feel healthy and strong, we can sometimes fall into the trap of mindless eating. We finish up the kids' pizza or suddenly discover that the handful of potato chips we had planned to eat has turned into an entire bag as we got caught up in our favorite sitcom. Sometimes it seems as if someone else is doing the eating—the food keeps going into our mouths, but our minds are on something else.

Of course, it's hard to pay attention to every bite we eat, but becoming more mindful will mean fewer binges, fewer calories, and less guilt. Fortunately, awareness is like a muscle. Use it, and it will get stronger. And as your awareness gets stronger, you'll find it's easier to stop eating when you're no longer hungry.

At your next meal or snack, I want you to actively pay attention to your body as you eat. This can be harder than it sounds, since we're usually paying attention to everything but what we're putting in our mouths. The TV, the kids, and the next thing you have to do at work or home may all be vying for your attention. If you've been keeping your food journal consistently for the past 5 weeks, you've already started to strengthen your awareness "muscle" as you recorded your hunger and fullness ratings. Now it's time to do something with that awareness. Now, when you start to feel full, I want you to put down your fork and leave the table.

At first this is going to be difficult, but if you stick with it, this practice becomes second nature. Here are some strategies to get you started.

Slow down. For some of us, it's been years since we had a meal where we ate slowly and focused on the food. We gulp down our meal or snack as fast as possible so we can get on to the next thing. Yet it takes 15 to 20 minutes for the brain to realize that the stomach is full—and we can do a lot of damage in those minutes. By making a point of slowing down, you'll enjoy your food more and eat less.

Turn off the TV, shut down the computer. Our lives are so busy that many of us wouldn't get through the day if we hadn't learned how to multitask. That's fine for many activities, but not for eating. When you eat while watching TV or working on the computer, you're not paying attention to your body, which means you'll probably eat right through your body's signals telling you it's full.

Quiz yourself. Mindless eating is made all the more dangerous when we're eating foods that aren't the healthiest choices to begin with. And let's face it, it's a lot easier to eat too many corn chips than it is to eat too many carrot sticks. So the next time you reach for a snack, pause to ask yourself the following questions. You may just discover that there's a better choice you could make—or even that you're not really hungry.

- Am I rushing to eat this food without thinking about my choices?
- How do I feel? Am I stressed, rushed, or tired?
- Is this food choice going to make me feel good 5 minutes from now?
- Is this food choice going to make me feel good an hour from now?

- Is there a chance I could be thirsty instead of hungry?
- Do I want to eat this quickly, before anyone sees me?
- Am I shutting down my awareness in order to eat this food?
- Will eating this food help me feel more balanced?
- Am I eating to reward myself for something?
- Am I eating to avoid working or having an uncomfortable conversation?

Say no to supersizing. Everyone loves a bargain, but the individual supersized portions some restaurants offer would be more appropriate for a family of four. And once they're on your tray, it's easy to polish them off, even though you'd probably never make such a huge portion for yourself at home. The best strategy is to stick with regular-size portions, then slow down and enjoy the smell, taste, and texture of your meal. If you do that, you'll be satisfied with the more reasonable serving size.

In restaurants that offer only one portion size, ask for a container as soon as your meal arrives. Then, before you start eating, decide how much you'll eat and package up the rest for lunch tomorrow.

Banish eating in your car. Certain places should be off-limits for eating, and the car is one of them. Do you find yourself pulling into a fast-food drive-thru, then mindlessly gobbling down the food as you drive to your next appointment or errand? Or perhaps you travel a lot for your job, and you've gotten in the habit of grabbing a quick snack from a convenience store to eat as you drive. This week, make an effort not to eat in your car. Even if you have to stop and sit for a few minutes, those extra minutes taken for yourself will bring a sense of calm and control to your day. And remember: The days you have no time to prepare your own meals are the days you should take extra care to eat food that supports you instead of food that will slow you down.

Close up the kitchen at night. The evening is a particularly dangerous time for mindless eating. It may be the first time all day you have to relax, and that often translates into a late-night binge. Before you head for the kitchen, though, ask yourself how you're going to feel tomorrow morning if you eat late at night. People who don't snack late at night tend to sleep better and wake up more easily—and, of course, they save on unneeded calories.

PLAN YOUR DAILY STRATEGY

There's an old saying that still holds true today: "If you fail to plan, you plan to fail." The strategies I've given you over the past 5 weeks are guaranteed to help you lose weight, support your workouts, and make you look and feel better. But they don't just happen: You've got to plan for success.

Each day, you should have a simple strategy of what you're going to eat and when you're going to eat it. You want to space out your meals, so that you never go more than a few hours without eating. Be sure to take your schedule, including your exercise routine, into consideration. I have a really early start to my day, so I'm usually having my second meal at the time some people are having their first. Remember that one size does not fit all. If you aren't very hungry in the morning, there's no rule that says you have to eat first thing. Listen to your body. You may like to be up for an hour before you have your first meal.

Keep in mind the commonsense strategies you have incorporated into your life as you create your plan.

Of course, you can have the greatest plan in the world, but if you open your refrigerator and the only item in there is leftover birthday cake, you're not going to get very far. So part of your planning is going to involve a trip to the grocery store. But before you get your car keys, you'll need to do a bit of preparation.

Review your journal. To help you decide what to purchase at the grocery store, look back at your food journal. It will provide a wealth of information for figuring out which foods work best for you, and which ones you should avoid.

Here are some of the questions you'll want to consider as you review your journal.

◆ How did my breakfast choices affect the rest of my day? Perhaps an egg-white omelette with spinach gave you the energy you needed to power through your day. Or maybe you felt better eating some fruit salad with a half cup of cottage cheese. Evaluate how what you ate for breakfast affected your choices throughout the rest of the day.

◆ What did I eat when I was truly hungry (as opposed to bored or stressed)? These are likely to be healthful foods you'll want to have on hand.

◆ What did I eat the days I felt the best? Try to pinpoint those foods that make you feel your best. For example, do salads make you feel in peak shape? Did you like having fruit to snack on? Keep what works for you in mind as you make your grocery list.

◆ Which healthful foods were most convenient for lunch? Was it a can of tuna? How about that leftover chicken breast? Or did you end up throwing it out at the end of the week?

◆ What foods do I tend to overeat? If you have a tendency to lose control around fat-free cookies, perhaps you can replace them with some fresh fruit or frozen fruit bars. If you tend to binge on certain foods, keep them out of the house.

Create a grocery list. Using what you've discovered from your food journal, write out your grocery list. Try to plan ahead for the week, so that you have at least a general idea of the meals and snacks you'll be eating each day. And be sure to include those foods that have proven to be successful for you over the last few weeks.

Also, keep in mind what you'll need to continue the strategies you've been learning over the past 5 weeks. Stock up on bottled water, if that's what you've been using to get your eight glasses a day. Do you need lemon or lime to go with that? Write it down.

You'll also want to stock up on fresh and frozen vegetables, so that you can continue to get lots of smart carbs. If you like fruit, skip the fruit juice and high-sugar fruits like bananas and dates, and instead plan to purchase those fruits that fill you up the most, like apples, oranges, pears, and berries.

Have you been getting enough healthy fats? Perhaps this is the week you try grilling some salmon or tuna. If you like nuts, try getting raw unsalted almonds to use in your salads or as a snack.

Finally, plan to buy some low-fat sources of protein, such as fish, soy, egg whites, chicken or turkey breast, low-fat dairy products, or lean cuts of meat.

Consider grocery store real estate. The healthiest aisles in the grocery store are the outer ones—the ones where they keep the fresh produce and the fish, chicken, and meat. You should be spending most of your time there.

Of course, this is *your* plan. I've never told you that you can't eat something you really want, and I'm not going to start now. Just use the strategies you've developed to make the smartest choices for you and your family. When you hit the middle aisles, try to remember your strategy of eating as close to the source as possible.

Before you put something in your grocery cart, read the label. Can you recognize the ingredients? Do they seem reasonable? If you're buying whole grain cereal and the first ingredient is sugar, you'll probably want to put that box back on the shelf. There are great whole grain cereals out there; you just have to read the labels.

Also, don't be misled by a colorful stamp on the package that says the product now contains less fat. The manufacturer might have taken out the fat but added more sugar. Or there might be so much fat in the product, taking out some doesn't make a dent.

Finally, ask yourself if the food you're considering is close to the source. Could you figure out where it comes from? How many steps of processing did this food need to get to the grocery shelf? Common sense will get you through the grocery store.

Give yourself easy access. Okay, you've made it through the grocery store and have selected food that both tastes good and is good for you. The last step to ensure your success is to make sure you have easy access to it—after all, what good is a refrigerator full of different varieties of fresh vegetables and fruit if you never take the time to prepare them? Too many of us leave the grocery store with the best of intentions, only to throw away scads of rotting lettuce, brown tomatoes, and moldy fruit a week later.

Here are some tips to ensure that the good food you bought will be the good food you end up eating.

- Have vegetables cut up and ready to eat in your refrigerator. Cut a whole bunch at once and store them in plastic containers. Or, if you're having a particularly busy week, buy some already sliced veggies from the grocery store salad bar.
- Hard-cook a dozen eggs at once so you'll have egg whites available to put in your salads or to have as a snack.
- Cook a few chicken breasts ahead of time and cut them into small strips. This way, you can easily prepare a meal with the already-cooked chicken breast.
- Do as my grandmother did. No matter what, she always had a bowl of fruit on the kitchen table. There was also fruit in the refrigerator, but seeing that bowl of fruit always gave us easy access to a healthy snack.

Prepare for those special circumstances.
Birthday parties, dinner out at a great restaurant, holiday get-togethers: These are some of the things that make life fun, but they can also be a challenge when you're trying to eat healthfully. Yet, once again, a little advance planning can make all the difference. Below are a few tips to get started. You'll notice that instead of bombarding you with a list of what you *can't* have, these tips are success-oriented by showing you what you *can* have. Use them to create an action plan that will have you sailing through special events without regretting your food choices.

- Keep a list of restaurants that have healthy choices, so you can quickly choose a restaurant when you're planning to go out to eat. You might even call a new restaurant ahead of time and ask them to fax you a menu, so you can make sure there will be healthful dishes for you to choose.
- Think water before wine. If you have to have a glass of wine, have a full glass of water first. It will fill you up and keep you from having a second glass of wine.
- If you're out at a restaurant, order the salmon or tuna instead of the steak. You increase your healthy fats while decreasing the bad ones by avoiding the steak. Or choose a grilled or baked chicken breast instead of fried chicken.
- Look for the dishes that are based on fresh vegetables. If you're going to have pizza no matter what, increase your vegetable intake by ordering fresh spinach and tomato on top. The extra fiber will also help fill you up.
- Order the side dish that traveled the shortest distance from the garden. The sautéed vegetables are certainly closer to the source than the deep-fried onion rings.
- Finally, if you really feel the need to splurge, you might want to work what I call "the 95 percent rule" into your eating strategies. This means that you eat well 95 percent of the time, and the other 5 percent, you allow yourself to indulge in whatever you please. Overall, you're still eating healthfully, and by knowing that you can have the occasional treat, you'll probably feel more satisfied, which means less of a chance that you'll have an unplanned binge.

PART FIVE

TRAINING LOGS

CORE

Core Basics Training Log

Date _____

Synergy Set 1	Reps/Breaths	Round 1	Round 2
Ball Towel Crunch	10–25 reps		
Diagonal Ball Crunch	10–25 reps each side		
Hangover Break	5 breaths		
Drape and Stretch	5 breaths		
Synergy Set 2			
Plank	5–15 breaths		
Back Extension	10–15 reps		
Cat Stretch	5 breaths		
Child's Pose	5 breaths		

Core Intermediate Training Log

Date _____

Synergy Set 1	Reps/Breaths	Round 1	Round 2
Triple-Count Crunch	10–15 reps		
Side Crunch on Ball	10–25 reps each side		
Hangover to the Side	5 breaths each side		
Synergy Set 2			
Plank on Ball	5–10 breaths		
Hyperextension on Ball	10–15 reps		
Drape and Stretch	5 breaths		
Knees to Chest	5 breaths		
Knees to Side	5 breaths each side		

Core Challenge Training Log

Date _____

Synergy Set 1	Reps/Breaths	Round 1	Round 2
Diagonal Crunch with Leg Lift	10–15 reps		
Roll-In	10–15 reps		
Super Side Stretch	5 breaths each side		

Synergy Set 2	Reps/Breaths	Round 1	Round 2
Windshield Wiper	10–15 reps each side		
Superwoman	10–15 reps		
Figure 4 Crunch	10 reps each side		
Figure 4 Stretch	5 breaths each side		
Lying Eagle	5 breaths each side		

Core Express Training Log

Date _____

Synergy Set 1	Reps/Breaths	Round 1	Round 2
Towel Crunch	10–20 reps		
Circle Crunch	10–15 reps each direction		
Double Crunch	10–20 reps		
Alternate Arms and Legs	5–10 reps each side		
Downward Dog	5 breaths		
Wide Child's Pose	5 breaths		

LOWER BODY

Lower-Body Basics Training Log

Date _____

Synergy Set 1	Reps/Breaths	Round 1	Round 2
Wide Squat	10–15 reps		
Quarterback Stretch	5 breaths		

Synergy Set 2			
Drop Lunge	10–15 reps each side		
Lunge Stretch	5 breaths each side		

Synergy Set 3			
Lying Abduction	15 reps each side		
Abductor Stretch	5 breaths each side		
Lying Adduction	15 reps each side		
Lying Cobbler	5 breaths		
Knees to Chest	5 breaths		

Lower-Body Intermediate Training Log

Date _____

Synergy Set 1	Reps/Breaths	Round 1	Round 2
Ball Squat	10–15 reps		
Lunge Stretch on Ball	5 breaths each side		

Synergy Set 2			
Bridge on Ball	10–15 reps		
Lying Hamstring Stretch with Ball	5 breaths		

Synergy Set 3			
Abduction on Ball	10–15 reps each side		
Adduction on Ball	10–15 reps each side		
Figure 4 on Ball	5 breaths each side		

Lower-Body Challenge Training Log

Date _____

Synergy Set 1		Round 1	Round 2
Walking Lunge	10–16 steps		
Wide Squat with Calf Raise	10–15 reps		
Deep Quarterback Stretch	5 breaths		
Stiff-Legged Deadlift	15 reps		
Standing Cross-Legged Bend	5 breaths each side		

Synergy Set 2			
One-Legged Bridge	10–15 reps each side		
Lying Stretch and Extend	5 breaths each side		
Lying Side Passé	10–15 reps each side		
Side Lift and Circle	5–10 circles each direction, each side		
Lying Eagle	5 breaths each side		

Lower-Body Express Training Log

Date _____

Synergy Set 1	Reps/Breaths	Round 1	Round 2
Around-the-World Squat	3 cycles of 4 reps		
Windmill Stretch	5 breaths each side		
Balance Bend	5–15 breaths		
Standing Forward Bend	5 breaths		

Synergy Set 2			
Express Leg Circles	5–10 reps each direction, each side		
One-Legged Stretch and Extend	5 breaths each side		

UPPER BODY

Upper-Body Basics Training Log

Date _____

Synergy Set 1	Reps/Breaths	Round 1	Round 2
Close-Grip Row	12 reps		
Prep Pushup	3 breaths each part, 3 times		
Easy-Open Stretch	5 breaths		

Synergy Set 2			
Lateral Raise	12 reps		
Standing Curl	12 reps		
One-Arm Triceps Kickback	12 reps each arm		
Back Stretch	5 breaths each part		

Upper-Body Intermediate Training Log

Date _____

Synergy Set 1	Reps/Breaths	Round 1	Round 2
Dumbbell Press on Ball	12 reps		
Chest Stretch	5 breaths		
Pullover on Ball	12 reps		
Pullover Stretch	5 breaths		

Synergy Set 2			
Lying Triceps Extension	12 reps		
Seated Triceps Stretch	5 breaths each arm		

Synergy Set 3			
Front Raise	12 reps		
Double-Delt Stretch	5 breaths		
Leaning Biceps Curl	12 reps		
Single-Arm Wall Stretch	5 breaths each arm		

Upper-Body Challenge Training Log

Date _____

Synergy Set 1		Round 1	Round 2
Fly and Press	12 reps each movement		
Up-and-Over Stretch	5 breaths		
Row on Ball	12 reps		
Side Stretch	5 breaths each side		

Synergy Set 2			
Y Rear Lateral	12 reps		
Eagle Arms	5 breaths each side		
Kickback on Ball	12 reps		
Cobra on Ball	5 breaths		
Angled Biceps Curl on Ball	12 reps		
Child's Pose on Ball	5 breaths		

Upper-Body Express Training Log

Date _____

Synergy Set 1	Reps/Breaths	Round 1	Round 2
Strong Curves Pushup	8–12 reps		
Bent-Over Row	12 reps		
Laced-Hands Stretch	5 breaths		

Synergy Set 2			
Double-Triceps Kickback	12 reps		
Standing Constant Curl	12 reps each arm		
Two-Part Arm Stretch	3 breaths each movement		

ACKNOWLEDGMENTS

I would like to thank the following people for their support and encouragement during the production of this book:

To my clients, students, and readers: Thank you for your dedication and hard work. You inspire me every day.

My extraordinary teachers: Christopher and Erika Hildebrandt, the first people I have ever met who expect more of me than I do. Your teaching, patience, and wisdom have made a profound impact on my life.

Montel Williams, thank you.

The best gym, the best trainers, the best equipment: Thank you, Max Pierre, Dennis Tan, and Gary Prince for providing New York City with the best Gold's Gym possible.

My family, East Coast division: You have all supported me unconditionally, and for that I am forever grateful. Special thanks to my mother, Linda Linguvic, who first inspired me to communicate through the written word. Regina, Angelo, Forrest, and Serena Bonolo, and Steve and Reiko Love, thank you.

My family, West Coast division: My father, Stanley Linguvic, who let me put my first weight set in the living room. Marlyne and Bill Schwartz, and Matt and Nicole Schwartz, thanks for welcoming me.

Connie Cincotta, Julie Lewit-Nirenberg, Laura Chonoles, Cherie Ward, Judy Greenbaum, Steve Florio, and Si Newhouse: It is training weather year-round.

The group of talented people at Rodale have taught me the true meaning of teamwork. Mariska van Aalst, my wonderful editor; Amy Kovalski, who is just brilliant; Tami Booth; Chris Gaugler; Karen Neely; Amy Morgan; Cathy Lee Gruhn; Amy Rhodes; Matthew Reigner; and all the rest of the excellent people at Rodale. Special thanks to Mary Lengle, who first introduced us all.

Thanks also to Mitch Mandel, the excellent photographer who took the beautiful photos in this book. Your attention to detail and patience are reflected in your outstanding work.

I'd also like to express my gratitude to Alice Martell, my wonderful agent, and to Howard Kaminsky, who introduced me to Alice. To Noni Rosenblatt, who helped me get those first ideas organized. Honor Scott, thanks for being such a good friend to us. And thanks to Jack, George, Bella, and Fitz for letting Griffin sleep over.

To Melanie McLaughlin, Diane Rappoport, Susan Henry, Jen Roe, Michelle Hinchliffe, Joe Pryor, Angela Lee, Nancy Goldman, Tania Ribalow, Amy Acton, and everyone else at the *Montel* show. And to Robin Hommel, a special salute for helping me work with all those wonderful *Body-Change* readers.

Beryl, Blix, Felix, Indy, and Griffin, you put it all in perspective.

Most of all, thank you, Kim. You are my heart and my home.

INDEX

Boldface page references indicate photographs. <u>Underscored</u> references indicate boxed text.

Grapes, 273
Grape tomatoes, 271
Greens, 271, <u>278</u>
Grocery list, 282–83

H

Hangover break, 30, **30**, 49, **49**
Hangover to the side, 48–49, **48–49**
Heart rate monitor, <u>18</u>, 19
Hunger
    mistaking for thirst, 265
    rating, 261–62
Hydration, 265
Hyperextension on ball, 52–53, **52–53**

I

Ice cream, 261, 274
Injury prevention, 239–40
Interval training, 20–21
Iron, 272, 275

J

Journal, food
    carrying, 260
    recording
        amounts of foods, 260–61
        feeling factor, 262–63
        food and drinks, 260
        fullness factor, 262
        hunger rating, 261–62
        time of meals and snacks, 261
    reviewing, 281–82
    selecting, 259–60
    template, 264
Juice, 266, 267, 270, 276

K

Kale, 271
Kickback
    on ball, 212–13, **212–13**
    double-triceps, 229, **229**
    one-arm triceps, 174–75, **174–75**,
        229

Knees to chest (stretch), 31, **31**, 55,
    55, 74, **74**, 107, **107**
Knees to side (stretch), 56–57, **56–57**,
    75, **75**

L

Label, food, 268
Laced-hands stretch, 228, **228**
Lamb, 275
Lateral raise, **170**, 170–71
Leaning biceps curl, **194**, 194–95
LeanLongandStrong.com (Web site),
    11
Lemon juice, 270, 276
Lengthening stretches
    for core
        cat stretch, 36–37, **36–37**, 88, **88**
        child's pose, 38, **38**
        downward dog, 88, **88**
        drape and stretch, 31, **31**, 54, **54**
        figure 4 stretch, 74, **74**
        hangover break, 30, **30**, 49, **49**
        hangover to the side, 48–49,
            48–49
        knees to chest, 31, **31**, 55, **55**,
            74, **74**, 107, **107**
        knees to side, 56–57, **56–57**, 75,
            75
        lying eagle, 75, **75**, 145, **145**
        super side stretch, 66–67, **66–67**
        wide child's pose, 89, **89**
    for lower body
        abductor stretch, 103, **103**
        deep quarterback stretch, 132,
            132
        figure 4 on ball, 122–23, **122–23**
        knees to chest, 107, **107**
        lunge stretch, 100–101,
            100–101
        lunge stretch on ball, 114–15,
            114–15
        lying cobbler, 106, **106**
        lying eagle, 145, **145**
        lying hamstring stretch with ball,
            118, **118**
        lying stretch and extend, 140–41,
            140–41
        one-legged stretch and extend,
            159, **159**

quarterback stretch, 96–97,
    96–97, 133, **133**
standing cross-legged bend,
    136–37, **136–37**
standing forward bend, 156–57,
    156–57
windmill stretch, 152–53,
    152–53
for upper body
    back stretch, 176–77, **176–77**
    chest stretch, 184, **184**
    child's pose on ball, 218, **218**
    cobra on ball, 214, **214**
    double stretch, 192–93, **192–93**
    eagle arms, 210–11, **210–11**
    easy-open stretch, 168–69,
        168–69
    laced-hands stretch, 228, **228**
    pullover stretch, 186, **186**
    seated triceps stretch, 188–89,
        188–89
    side stretch, 206–7, **206–7**
    single-arm wall stretch, 196–97,
        196–97
    two-part arm stretch, **232**,
        232–33
    up-and-over stretch, 204, **204**
Lettuce, 271, 276, 283
Lower-body exercises
    abduction on ball, 119, **119**
    adduction on ball, 120, **120**
    around-the-world squat, 150–51,
        150–51
    balance bend, 154–55, **154–55**
    ball squat, 112–13, **112–13**
    bridge, 117, **117**, 135, **135**, 139,
        139
    bridge on ball, 116–17, **116–17**
    drop lunge, 98–99, **98–99**, 129,
        129
    express leg circles, 158, **158**
    lying abduction, 102, **102**, 119,
        119
    lying adduction, 104–5, **104–5**,
        121, **121**
    lying side passé, 142–43, **142–43**
    one-legged bridge, 138–39,
        138–39
    side lift and circle, 144, **144**
    stiff-legged deadlift, 134–35,
        134–35